ION

16/-

WILFRED OWEN
A Critical Study

WILFRED OWEN
A Critical Study

D. S. R. WELLAND

*Professor of American Literature in
the University of Manchester*

1969

CHATTO & WINDUS

LONDON

15,733

Published by
Chatto & Windus Ltd
42 William IV Street
London W.C.2

*

Clarke, Irwin & Co Ltd
Toronto

First published 1960
Second impression 1968
Third impression 1969

SBN 7011 1201 8

SBN Non-Net 7010 0328 6

© D.S.R. WELLAND 1960
Lowe & Brydone (Printers) Ltd
London

For
JOAN and MICHAEL

Contents

Acknowledgements

Some parts of this book are based on material that has already appeared in print elsewhere and I am grateful to the editors of the following periodicals for permission to re-publish it here: *The Times Literary Supplement* which, on 15 and 22 June 1956, published material incorporated in Chapters III and VII; *The Review of English Studies* which in July 1950 published an article from which the present Chapter VI is condensed; and *Northern Review* (Montreal) which in October/November 1953 printed, under the title 'Wilfred Owen: Poetry, Pity and Prophecy' a general essay on Owen.

For permission to quote extracts from copyright poems in this book my thanks are due to the following: Mr. Harold Owen and Messrs. Chatto & Windus for the quotations from Wilfred Owen; Mr. Edmund Blunden and Messrs. Macmillan for the extract from Mr. Blunden's '*Premature Rejoicing*'; Mrs. Yeats and Messrs. Macmillan for the extract from W. B. Yeats's 'On Being Asked for a War Poem'; The Society of Authors and Dr. John Masefield, O.M., for the extract from 'Forget'; The Bodley Head for the extract from 'The Iron Music' by Ford Madox Hueffer; and the authors' representatives and Messrs. Sidgwick Jackson Ltd. for the extracts from 'Failure' from *The Collected Poems of Rupert Brooke* and 'Gonnehem' from *A Gloucestershire Lad* by F. W. Harvey.

D. S. R. W.

Preface

THIS book is designed for the reader already familiar with the text of Wilfred Owen's poetry and with Mr Edmund Blunden's memoir of the poet prefatory to the standard edition of his poems. As the title indicates, it is concerned with Owen's work, it makes no pretence at biography, and it does not claim, except, perhaps, in some questions of textual variants, to be definitive. The final chapter in particular is intended to do little more than make suggestions for further reading and comparison.

My interest in Owen, dating from undergraduate days and intensified by my own more limited experience of war between 1939 and 1945, has been of too long a duration and has involved me with too many people for me to be able comprehensively to acknowledge every indebtedness; and I assure all those whose names are not recorded below—not least among them the many students with whom I have discussed Owen's work—that I am by no means unmindful of or ungrateful for the help that in their several ways they have so readily given me.

The book is based on a thesis for which the degree of Doctor of Philosophy in the University of Nottingham was awarded in 1951; in the research preparatory to that work I was most liberally helped by Mr Siegfried Sassoon and Mr Edmund Blunden who not only made available to me letters and other material in their possession but also discussed most fully with me my impressions and conclusions at all stages of the work. Sir Osbert Sitwell also allowed me access to his collection of Owen manuscripts and has graciously consented to my quoting one of them in this book; both he and Dame Edith Sitwell have at all times been most helpful to me. The poet's brother and literary executor, Mr Harold Owen, has very generously allowed me not only to quote extensively from the published poems but also to reproduce for the first time several extracts from hitherto unpublished pieces; for this privilege I am particularly grateful. I also owe a great debt to Wilfred Owen's cousin, Mr E. Leslie Gunston, for much personal kindness as well as for his generosity in allowing me to consult the letters, manuscripts and photographs in his possession. To Mr C. Day Lewis, Mr Robert Graves, Mr George Scott Moncrieff, Professor Louis Bonnerot of the Université de Caën, and Mr W. Kay, sometime Borough Librarian of Oswestry, I should also like to express my thanks. Finally, I wish to record my gratitude to Professor V. de S. Pinto of the University of Nottingham who not only inspired my interest in Owen but who, in the years since then, has been an unfailing friend and counsellor in this and many other undertakings. For the imperfections of the present work, none of these benefactors can, of course, be held in any way responsible.

NOTTINGHAM   D. S. R. WELLAND

SEPTEMBER 1959

CHAPTER ONE

Poetry and the First World War

'THE lamps are going out all over Europe; we shall not see them lit again in our lifetime.' When Sir Edward Grey as Foreign Secretary used those words on the third of August 1914 to prepare the House of Commons for the declaration of war that was made on the following day, he may not himself have realised with what prophetic accuracy he spoke. Few men have so punctually or so dramatically pronounced the epitaph of an era, yet many of his hearers must have been more impressed by the solemnity of his utterance than by his almost preternatural sense of history; neither he nor they could fully foresee the emotive overtones that for later generations were to cluster round the phrase 'before the War'. King George V had already reigned for four years but it is August 1914 rather than his accession that marks the end of what we have come to think of as 'Edwardian England'. Grey's recognition of this has been subsequently endorsed by such men of letters as Sir Osbert Sitwell, Siegfried Sassoon, E. M. Forster and L. P. Hartley whose retrospective writings have characterised that period as an Indian summer when even the weather was more glorious than it has ever been since. Memory may have intensified the metaphorical, as well as the literal, sunshine of that 'great morning' or that 'weald of youth' as they variously described it, but there is no likelihood of a comparable glamour being cast by recollection over the 'long weekend' between the wars, much less over the uneasy nuclear- shadowed years since 1945.

For the literary historian, however, the Great War is less

clearly defined as a turning point. It provided many writers with a new kind of material which they utilised with varying success during the war and more effectively when the passage of time had set it in perspective: the late 1920's and early 30's produced the best memoirs and novels about the war but these works are more important for the newness of their content than for any radical change in their literary form. The post-war novelists whose work showed most originality and did most to alter the pattern of fiction are James Joyce, D. H. Lawrence and Virginia Woolf, writers on whose work the War had far less direct effect than had the deepened understanding of the human personality that resulted from advances in the study of psychology.

Similarly we can now see that some of the most influential poetic movements of the first quarter of the century owed little of their impetus to the War: although Imagism might have developed differently had T. E. Hulme not been killed in 1917, its direction had already been determined by the poetry of Ezra Pound, and although the War was in large part responsible for the breakdown of values diagnosed in 'The Waste Land' it was not from the War but from Pound, *il miglior fabbro* of the dedication, that Eliot learnt how to write. Meanwhile W. B. Yeats was deliberately keeping the War out of his poetry (except for the version of his 'Irish Airman' poem unpublished until after his death):

> I think it better that in times like these
> A poet's mouth be silent, for in truth
> We have no gift to set a statesman right
>> ('On being asked for a War Poem')

This idea Yeats was later to elevate into a critical principle in his preface to the *Oxford Book of Modern Verse* and yet during the War years his own style of writing was undergoing a change as drastic as that in many of the soldier-poets he excluded from that anthology. Events in Ireland, culminating in the Easter Rising in 1916, had much to do with this, but Yeats's progress from 'Celtic twilight' Romanticism to what, in 'A Coat', he defines as the greater enterprise of 'walking naked' is not to be ascribed solely to his feelings for Ireland. For various reasons several of his contemporaries were beginning to recognise how effete the Romantic tradition was becoming. As early as 1908 J. M. Synge, seeing the need for what he called 'the strong things of life' in poetry, had written 'It may almost be said that before verse can be human again it must learn to be brutal'. Eight years later D. H. Lawrence was writing in a letter to Catherine Carswell:

> The essence of poetry with us in this age of stark and unlovely actualities is a stark directness, without a shadow of a lie, or a shadow of deflection anywhere. Everything can go, but this stark, bare, rocky directness of statement, this alone makes poetry today.

Meanwhile in 1915 the prefatory manifesto to *Some Imagist Poets* had announced the determination of that group also 'To produce poetry that is hard and clear, never blurred nor indefinite', thus striving to fulfil Hulme's earlier prediction 'A period of hard, dry, classical verse is coming'.

Thus, although these new conceptions of poetry coincide chronologically with the Great War they were not necessarily nor in all cases directly occasioned by it: that several of them originated before the War is a salutary warning against too facile a dovetailing of literary and social history. The progress of poetry in the twentieth century can be conveniently epitomised in the work of W. B. Yeats alone, but it can be seen with equal clarity elsewhere, not least in the poetry written during and about the First World War, with some of which this book is concerned. The validity of the convenient term 'war poetry' has been challenged by Yeats and others, and it should be clear from what has been said above that its use in the following pages is not intended to denote a form of poetry *sui generis*, existing in a vacuum distinct from other poetry of the age. In the same way, to speak of Wilfred Owen as a war poet is true only as long as the phrase is used to denote one of the sources of and formative influences on his work: it is grotesquely untrue if it is used, as it sometimes has been, to imply that it was only the War that made him a poet. To approach Owen's poetry, as I wish to, by first tracing briefly the development of 'war poetry' is to place him in a context and to provide a perspective in which one aspect of the magnitude of his achievement may be better estimated, not to isolate him from the tradition of English poetry to which, as I shall hope to show, he both owed and contributed so much.

II

When war was declared in August 1914 the mood of the nation had little in common with the sobriety of Sir Edward Grey, much less with Bernard Shaw's later view of 'cultured, leisured Europe before the War' as 'Heartbreak House'. Whole-hearted certainty in the righteousness of the cause reinforced an exaggerated but long-standing faith in the infallibility of British military and naval power and produced a buoyant and easy confidence that the war would be 'over by Christmas'; the campaign took on the nature of a crusade in more serious moments, while in lighter moods it seemed an exciting and vaguely glorious adventure. That attitude was destined not to last very long (although there was a less excusable recurrence of a mood not wholly dissimilar in 1939) but it did provide the stimulus for a good deal of verse that has dated very rapidly because of its authors' unfamiliarity with their subject. The last major European war in which this country had been involved was the Crimean, and the Crimea was geographically far enough removed for an outstanding military blunder at Balaclava to undergo, at the hands of Tennyson, a metamorphosis into a glorification of English valour and prowess that is still exciting to many. Between 1856 and the Boer War the British Army had been engaged only in campaigns against native troops in various parts of Africa and India so remote that report could magnify and embellish the event out of recognition on the journey home, and could lose sight of such embarrassing factors as the disparity of weapons between the two forces. Matthew Arnold's brother William had been a lieutenant in India and had recorded his first-hand impressions of the less glorious aspects of the Frontier campaigns in a novel *Oakfield*, published in 1854; that it was never a popular favourite is not wholly attributable to its literary shortcomings. So, too, with the Boer War: Kipling became famous for 'The Absent-Minded Beggar' and 'Bobs' with a public that conveniently overlooked his presentation, in such poems as 'Stellenbosch' and 'That Day', of the less creditable side of war.

Moreover, the search by Synge, Yeats, Lawrence, the Imagists and others for new and revitalised poetic forms is tacit evidence of the debilitated condition of pre-1914 poetry which in the hands of such poets as William Watson was undistinguished in its mediocrity. Even some of the Georgian group, whom Edward Marsh tried in 1912 to present as a new and exciting movement, seemed incapable of treating poetically anything more than the most ephemeral of trivia or, when they did attempt the more serious, falsified it by the hollowness of their pseudo-Romantic rhetoric. In short, for the poet in 1914 meditating a poem on the War, every precedent seemed to encourage an attitude and an idiom that can best be designated 'bardic'. A host of poets, mostly minor, hastened with a zeal that outran both their ability and their discretion to proclaim the rightness of the national cause in clarion tones. *Songs and Sonnets for England in Wartime*[*] is an anthology representative of their work. It must in fairness be admitted that much of this verse was originally written for publication in the national press in August and September 1914 so that its jingoistic journalese is that much more excusable, but certainly its literary merit is very slight. Hardy's 'Men Who March Away' (here entitled 'Song of the Soldiers') and Kipling's 'For All We Have and Are' are its only memorable poems. Self-righteousness and a stiff upper lip draw strength from a confident reliance upon divine approval:

> For a Europe's flouted laws
>   We the sword reluctant drew,
> Righteous in a righteous cause:
>   Britons, we WILL see it through!
>   (R. M. Freeman: from 'The War Cry')

The frequency of reference to Nelson, Drake, and Waterloo reflects the inadequate conception of the nature of modern war, but atrocity stories are already being used to stimulate nationalist frenzy against the Kaiser who is blamed for

> Villages burned down to dust,
> Torture, murder, bestial lust,
> Filth too foul for printer's ink,
> Crimes from which the apes would shrink.
>   (Barry Pain: from 'The Kaiser and God')

[*]John Lane: The Bodley Head: 1914.

Perhaps the clearest and most pathetic expression of the 1914 spirit in this anthology is to be found in a poem by R. E. Vernède, 'The Call':

> Lad, with the merry smile and the eyes
>   Quick as a hawk's and clear as the day,
> You who have counted the game the prize,
>   Here is the game of games to play.
>   Never a goal—the captains say—
> Matches the one that's needed now:
>   Put the old blazer and cap away—
> England's colours await your brow.

Almost forty at the outbreak of war, Vernède was no callow young enthusiast, but his sense of duty led him to enlist as an infantry private. He later served as a subaltern with the Rifle Brigade on the Western Front where he was wounded in 1916 and killed in action in the following April, but not before his attitude to war had been drastically revised, as his published *Letters to His Wife* indicate. In 1916 he wrote to her:

> I feel rather doubtful as to whether I should tell you quite the unpleasant side like this; but I think it's rather good that nowadays, when women have so much influence, they should not be fooled with the rosy side of things only. I don't think I'm using my imagination. At any rate I'm willing to bet that not one of the men but would have given a good deal to be out of it.

Wilfred Owen's letters home in 1917 and 1918 show an awareness even fuller and more sensitive than this of the need for a total honesty to experience and he had the opportunity to transmute this into poetry in a way that Vernède did not; nevertheless, though Owen could not have known of Vernède's letters, it would be unjust, on the basis of 'The Call' to overstate the difference between their poetic aims. Owen was in Bordeaux until 1915 and thus missed the first 'bardic' flood, but one of the very few places where I have seen a copy of Vernède's *War Poems and Other Verses* (1917) is among the small library of Owen's books that his family have carefully preserved as he left them. This and a copy of *The Pageant of War* by Lady Margaret Sackville (to whom Sassoon had introduced him in Edinburgh) establish Owen's interest in some aspects of 'bardic' poetry, while the presence also of *1914 and Other Poems* by Rupert Brooke suggests the parallel between Vernède and a poet who had less time than he for second thoughts about this 'game of games'.

It is still sometimes necessary to remind both Brooke's admirers and his detractors—and there seem to be very few readers who are not decisively in one of these camps—how little he really saw of the war. Technically so much superior to many of these 'bardic' poets, Brooke is almost the only one who might have developed into an artist comparable to Owen. To compare them, as is often done, on the basis of *1914 and Other Poems* is misleading because of the totally different nature of the experience each is recording. How well Brooke crystallised in a few memorable lines what many people not only wanted to feel but did feel is borne out by the number of non-specialist readers for whom even today war poetry means only his five sonnets and a stanza, popularised by Armistice Day usage, from a poem that comparatively few of them would know to be Laurence Binyon's 'For the Fallen'. There is, as Mr John Lehmann claimed in a broadcast in 1944, 'under the surface brilliance a corrupting glibness' in Brooke's poetry and, when he writes of death, 'something almost pathetic in the way in which his mind sheers off the reality of the fact' but a similar

quality even more prominent in Owen's juvenilia was caut-
erised by his imaginative response to experience as Brooke's
might well have been also. 'Bardic' poetry, though it is still
capable of resuscitation, has fallen into a disrepute largely
justifiable because so much of it is just bad poetry built on
the hollowest of rhetoric—and I have not tried to illustrate
the worst excesses of it here—but with the exception of
Hardy's 'Men Who March Away' and Kipling's 'For All
We have and Are' Brooke's sonnets are its best flowering.

III

If Brooke had lived, and if his development had paralleled
that of war poetry in general, what would have been its
pattern? By 1915, although 'bardic' poetry continued to
appear in the national press, the arm-chair poets with their
hortatory rhetoric were no longer the only voices. An increasing number of young men like Brooke, not professional
soldiers but volunteers who had gone straight from school
or college, were finding themselves in France on active service, learning—those of them who lived long enough—to
adjust themselves to conditions so unimaginably alien to
anything they had known that their only consolation lay in
memories and dreams. It was of these, in snatched moments,
that they made poetry, and it was these that their poetry in
its turn nourished. Not often does their work attain any
high literary standard: generally it is the poetry that in more
normal circumstances they would have contributed to their
school or college magazine transposed to a war-time setting. Short nature-descriptions with a French instead of an
English background, personal love-lyrics which acquire a
deeper poignancy from enforced separation and often from
the later untimely death of the writer; occasionally a somewhat enhanced description of the battlefield or the writer's

feelings before an attack: examples will come readily to the mind of anyone familiar with anthologies published between, say, 1915 and 1930.* Because these poets are actuated primarily by a personal impetus, because war is incidental to their poetry rather than integral, it seems appropriate to designate this the 'personal phase' of war poetry.

It is a recognisable lyric impulse that gives rise to such a poem as that of F. W. Harvey's which ends:

> Unruffled peace the farm encloses—
> I wonder if beneath that tree,
> The meditating hens still be?
> Are the white walls now gay with roses?
> Does the small fountain yet run free?
> I wonder if the dog still dozes . . .
> Some day we must go back to see.

The reader who half expected the final line to run 'And is there honey still for tea?' can hardly be blamed. That this poem should have been inspired by a Belgian hamlet (it is called 'Gonnehem') is pure accident: the writer would have found himself another Grantchester in England had he not happened to be in Belgium, and in spite of its title it is really as much a poem of homesickness as is, for example, Ford Madox Hueffer's 'The Iron Music' from which this stanza comes:

> Dust and corpses in the thistles
> Where the gas-shells burst like snow,
> And the shrapnel screams and whistles
> On the Bécourt road below,
> And the High Wood bursts and bristles
> Where the mine-clouds foul the sky . . .

* The examples discussed on pp 20–22 will all be found in *An Anthology of War Poems* edited by Frederick Brereton (Collins, 1930).

> But I'm with you up at Wyndcroft,
> Over Tintern on the Wye.

Although dated 1916, this is clearly a poem where experience counts for less than day-dreams: the 'corpses in the thistles' are not imaginatively realised, any more than are the gas-shells (as the inadequacy of the perfunctory simile of snow reveals), and the whole scene makes no sharp impression on the reader at all.

Something of the 1914 spirit survives in these poets and as they idealise their homesickness so they continue to invest death with an alien and heroic glamour, although death is becoming less abstract and more personalised for them than for the 'bardic' school. (A reliable guide to war poetry could be written in terms of changes in poetic attitudes to death.) This emerges in the opening stanza of the well-known 'Into Battle' by Julian Grenfell, one of the few poets of the Regular Army:

> The naked earth is warm with spring,
>   And with green grass and bursting trees
> Leans to the sun's gaze glorying,
>   And quivers in the sunny breeze:
> And life is colour and warmth and light,
>   And a striving evermore for these;
> And he is dead who will not fight;
>   And who dies fighting has increase.

Later in the same poem comes a hint of the fatalism that, often subconsciously accepted, buoyed up so many soldiers of both wars:

> Nor lead nor steel shall reach him, so
>   That it be not the Destined Will.

Sometimes this produces the apparently casual indifference to death of C. H. Sorley's 'Route March':

All the hills and vales along
Earth is bursting into song,
And the singers are the chaps
Who are going to die perhaps.

Sometimes it produces the sort of wry epitaph W. W. Gibson provides in 'The Joke':

. . . but as he spoke
A rifle cracked . . .
And now God knows when I shall hear the rest.

However, a comparison of such poems with Owen's 'The Next War' will disclose subtle but significant differences between this attitude and his more imaginative and critical re-creation of it in a poem that makes articulate the unspoken creed of many while at the same time commenting on it with a characteristic mixture of detachment and pity. Similarly this sort of poetry uses sentiment in a more obvious, less disciplined manner than Owen at his best. Alan Seeger's 'I Have a Rendezvous with Death' illustrates this by its very title, as well as by such lines as

It may be he shall take my hand
And lead me into his dark land
And close my eyes and quench my breath.

An even better-known example is John McCrae's 'In Flanders Fields':

If ye break faith with us who die
We shall not sleep, though poppies grow
In Flanders fields.

Owen's development of a somewhat similar theme in 'Strange Meeting' is not merely the work of a better poet but the product of a more mature vision and a fuller experience of the nature of war.

In September 1916 Erskine MacDonald published *Soldier Poets* edited by Galloway Kyle, in a cloth edition and a paperback 'Trench Edition'. Sub-titled 'Songs of the Fighting Men', this collection of poems hitherto unpublished in book form was announced by the publishers as 'The most significant literary volume connected with the war: a revelation and an inspiration: of great individual and historic interest and value'. The present-day reader will find its interest primarily historic. Of its twenty-four contributors the only one whose subsequently-collected works still command attention (though not as much as they merit) is Charles Hamilton Sorley; Grenfell's is probably the only other name likely to be known to the general reader. Some of the poems are so banal, and occasionally so near to bathos, that quotation would be unkind; many are remarkable only for the inappropriateness of their heavily-accented jogtrot metre to the meditative note that they attempt, or for a diction elevated, anachronistic and 'poetic' in the worst sense. Some, such as those by Dyneley Hussey, have a certain charm and an accomplishment in the Georgian manner as the ending of his sonnet 'Security' suggests:

> And, over all, the jade hills, windy, wide:
> These will I seek that they may shed on me
> The peacefulness of their security.

The formula of 'Grantchester' and 'The Great Lover' comes perilously near to being worked to death in this volume and the whole idiom is too derivative, too retrospective, to individualise the poems or even to counteract the nostalgia of their sentiment. The occasional glimpses of ugliness, notably in the work of the Canadian private, H. Smalley Sarson, show some observation and, as in 'The Village', some attempt at an objective realism but they are untouched by the deeper imaginative insight that characterises the work of Sassoon and Owen. The relationship between this poetry of the 'personal' phase and that of the 'bardic' is indicated by the editor's prefatory reference to the 'unity of spirit, of exultant sincerity and unconquerable idealism that makes the reader very proud and very humble'. The emphasis is shifting from the righteousness of the crusade to the knightliness of the crusader. *Soldier Poets* is none the less a convenient epitome of the scores of volumes by individual writers published, many of them posthumously, between 1915 and the early twenties.

Commenting on some of these in 1917 an anonymous critic in the *Nation* observed 'It is their grim and shattering destiny, their tragedy, rather than the destiny and tragedy of war that is revealed', and concluded that poetry 'is unable to cope with or contain war'. Owen implied a similar criticism in October 1918 when he wrote to Sassoon for two copies of his *Counter-Attack*, explaining 'One is for the Adjutant—who begged a book of Erskine MacD.'s *Soldier Poets* which I had with me—because I met one of these amalgamations at the Base'. The inference from this and the next sentence (grammatically something of a *non sequitur*) is that the copy of *Counter-Attack* was intended as a corrective to the impression of *Soldier Poets* from which Owen was already converting the Adjutant: it is a pity that we have no record of Owen's reaction to Galloway Kyle's fatuous claim for his volume that

> The note of pessimism and decadence is absent. . . . The soldier poets leave the maudlin and the mock-heroic, the gruesome and fearful handling of Death and his allies to the neurotic civilian who stayed behind to gloat on imagined horrors and inconveniences and anticipate the uncomfortable demise of friends.

Certainly none of the numerous poets of this phase could be cited in refutation of the *Nation*'s conclusion that 'no great poet has set his mind to modern war and brought it under his dominion'. Nevertheless poets of this quality were already at work; they and others were to constitute the third and most significant phase of war poetry, the phase in which Owen is of central importance..

IV

The transition from the second to the third phase is best studied in the works of Edmund Blunden, Robert Graves, and the less famous Arthur Græme West. Their work at first would seem to place them in the 'personal' category but they survived many of their contemporaries and an increased familiarity with war increased their sensibility. Blunden's 'Premature Rejoicing' is a useful pointer to the changes; a fragment of dialogue between (presumably) two officers, it visualises one indicating Thiepval Wood—a bitterly contested piece of land—to the other and picturing for him Titania, at present asleep in a dugout in the wood, finding herself once more mistress of its glades ten years hence. Many other poets of the time would have been content to end the poem there, but it is Blunden's characteristic additional comment that gives the poem its point:

> The burnt rubbish you've just seen
> Won't beat the Fairy Queen;
>   All the same, it's a shade too soon
>   For you to scribble rhymes
>   In your army book
>   About those times;
>   Take another look;
> That's where the difficulty is, over there.

The difference in tone and diction between this and all the other passages so far quoted is indicative, especially in the last two lines, of the more direct, colloquial immediacy that begins to replace bardic rhetoric and the personal lyric. By 1916 poets and many others were beginning to 'take another look' at the war and to realise where the 'difficulty' was. The illusions of 1914 were being rapidly dissipated: in spite of the church's continued support for the war, many fighting men were become less and less convinced that it was entirely a crusade; the army which was to have had the war 'over by Christmas' seemed bogged down—literally as well as meta-phorically—and the disaster of the Somme campaign of 1916 when 60,000 casualties were sustained on the first day of the battle had, to say the least of it, a sobering effect. It is not coincidence that the major poets of this final phrase were all, like Vernède, involved in the fighting on the Somme, and the proper names that crowd their poems—Thiepval Wood, Bapaume, Mametz, the Ancre, Fricourt, Festubert, Martin-puisch, Beaumont Hamel, and Jacob's Ladder—all belong to this sector. There were other sources of irritation, inevitable perhaps in modern war, but not likely to foster a spirit of tolerance in the infantryman: governmental muddle and staff incompetence were frequently distorted and exaggerated by rumour, but the rumour too often had an uncom-fortable basis in such facts as the shortage of artillery am-munition when it was most needed and the attacks that were repulsed by enemy forces stronger than had been expected. Idealism suffered one of its most serious set-backs, too, when details became known of the secret treaties that had led to the entry of Italy into the war in 1915; the concessions Great Britain had made to outbid Austria for Italian support not only placed a severe strain on relations with our French and Russian allies but in their calculated mercenariness outraged the susceptibilities of many patriots at home and in the forces. The soldier fought on—there seemed no alternative and the war had to be won—but the earlier sense of consecrated purpose was no longer strong enough to blind him to the bestiality, the horror and the appalling waste with which he was surrounded. Circumstances compelled him to 'take another look'.

In Blunden's poem on an attack (variously entitled 'Zero' or more ironically 'Come on, my lucky lads!') the dawn is no longer the encouraging token of victory that it would have been for poets only a year earlier; it has become a display of alien beauty set in rather bad taste as a backcloth to the more immediate devastation; against it a young subaltern awaits zero hour with an almost cynically resigned conception of his 'heritage' in terms very different from Brooke's. In the correspondence columns of the *Nation* in 1921 Blunden took Middleton Murry to task for remarking in a review of Owen's poems that the poetry of the war 'had to record not what the war did to men's bodies and senses, but what it did to their souls'. Blunden's comment was terse: 'The effect on the soul depended very closely on what happened to the body. We did not leave our bodies at the transport lines'. On this realisation is built not only Blunden's own poetry but that of Graves, Sassoon, Rosenberg, Owen—in short, of all the poets of this third phase of war poetry, the phase of protest.

The change of attitude towards the war is documented very fully in a number of prose memoirs of which Græme West's *Diary of a Dead Officer* was one of the few written at the time. Others came later. C. E. Montague's *Disenchantment* (1922), Blunden's *Undertones of War* (1928), Robert Graves's *Goodbye to All That* (1929), Sassoon's *Siegfried's Journey* (1945) all tell a similar story, a story that had received fictional dress in Richard Aldington's *Death of a Hero* (1929), Sassoon's *Memoirs of An Infantry Officer* (1930) and *Sherston's Progress* (1936), and in many others. It is a story at its mildest of disillusion and at its strongest of active opposition to the conduct of the war. Robert Graves refers to a movement of overt pacifism in late 1916 in which were prominent Bertrand Russell, Clive Bell, Lady Ottoline Morell and her husband, Lytton Strachey, and, among writers in the army, Osbert and Sacheverell Sitwell, Herbert Read, Siegfried Sassoon, Wilfred Owen and himself, 'none of whom now believed in the war'. The inclusion of Owen in this list suggests that Mr Graves has inadvertently antedated it, though probably only by a few months, and what each of these people understood by 'pacifism' would be far from identical. To ascribe to this 'movement' too wide an influence or too large a membership would be a mistake, but the columns of the *Nation* for this period, when it was more than once threatened with suppression, prove the existence of a vocal opposition to war in general and that war in particular. In February 1918 the *Nation* published an unsigned article entitled 'The Joy of Battle' attacking 'the romantic lie in such phrases' and ending:

> Let poets and writers and artists and all other soldiers of our time be allowed freely to describe the actual truth of war as they have seen it. Only so, if at all, can some check be laid upon that idealising habit which throws the attractive and picturesque glamour of time over wars but lately endured, just as moss and ferns encumber a ruined dungeon with their effeminate greenery.

A month earlier the *Nation* had printed a poem called 'Miners' above the signature of a young poet, two more of whose poems ('Futility' and 'Hospital Barge at Cérisy') were to appear in the same columns in June. These were the only poems of Owen's to receive national publication in his lifetime and the author of 'The Joy of Battle' could not have known how closely he had paraphrased in that passage the aims that Owen had already proposed to himself. Nor was Owen by any means the only poet and writer attempting by graphic fidelity in rendering his own experience to bring home to those with no first-hand knowledge of it, the true nature of modern war and thus to protest against 'man's inhumanity to man'. For some, such as Sassoon, protest seemed to demand the sting of satire; for Owen it necessitated the exercise of pity and thus brought into play in his poetry one of his dominant personal qualities; for all, it involved a relentless, uncompromising honesty, and all were, in their own ways, engaged in what the title of Sassoon's 1918 volume of poems called for: *Counter-Attack*. Poetry had progressed from rhetorical welcoming of war through passive resignation to an ardent rejection of it: this was a different sort of crusade and one for which Owen was singularly well qualified.

Similarly, though it lies outside the scope of this book, painting was already attempting what the writer in the *Nation* had asked of it. C. R. W. Nevinson had been recording since 1915 the domination of the soldier by the machine, the suffering of the civilian victims of shell-fire and air-raids, the grim squalor of casualty clearing stations; in 1918 he was obliged by official intervention to withdraw 'The Paths of Glory' from exhibition because of its stark portrayal of dead men caught in wire. While Nevinson painted war as, in the words of one of his critics, 'martial mechanism and monotonous monochrome . . . noisy and nefarious, dreary and disgusting', an even greater painter, Paul Nash, wrote a letter in November 1917 containing this passage:

I have seen the most frightful nightmare of a country more conceived by Dante or Poe than by nature, unspeakable, utterly indescribable. In the fifteen drawings I have made I may give you some vague idea of its horror. . . . Sunset and sunrise are blasphemous, they are mockeries to man, only the black rain out of the bruised and swollen clouds all through the bitter black of night is a fit atmosphere in such a land. The rain drives on, the stinking mud becomes more evilly yellow, the shell-holes fill up with green-white water, the roads and tracks are covered in inches of slime, the black, dying trees ooze and sweat and the guns never cease. They alone plunge overhead tearing away the rotting tree stumps, breaking the plank roads, striking down horses and mules, annihilating, maiming, maddening they plunge into the grave which is this land; one huge grave and cast upon it the poor dead. It is unspeakable, godless, hopeless. I am no longer an artist interested and curious. I am a messenger who will bring back word from the men who are fighting to those who want the war to go on for ever. Feeble, inarticulate will be my message, but it will have a better truth and may it burn their lousy souls.

Powerful as this is, its descriptive vividness pales rapidly beside the drawings to which it refers or such oil paintings as 'The Menin Road' and 'We Are Making a New World'. To look at the reproduction of these in the memorial volume *Paul Nash*★ is not only to see a pictorial equivalent to such poems of Owen's as 'The Show', 'Dulce et Decorum Est' and 'Strange Meeting' but to appreciate through the comparison a truth even more important about the work of both. It is best expressed by John Rothenstein when he says of Nash:

★Ed. Margot Eates (Lund Humphries, 1948). The letter quoted above is included in the essay by John Rothenstein in this book of which mention is also made below.

It is no injustice to the others to say that none of them interpreted the landscape of the Western Front so incisively, with such poetic intensity or with such severe economy as Paul Nash. Out of the chaos and the squalor he made an ordered poetry of form, which, even at those moments when it seemed most arbitrary, in fact never relaxed its hold upon objective reality. This innately gentle artist may be said to have discovered the full poetic potentialities of modern warfare.

The same paradox is true of Owen, who in his different medium is also an innately gentle artist who has schooled himself, through his firm hold on objective reality, to make out of ugliness a poetry with its own kind of beauty. That Owen should have proved that poetry can 'cope with and contain war' is of some historic significance but little more. If we over-emphasise his impassioned protest against war, we must logically, in the light of subsequent European history, see him as an idealist who failed signally to achieve his end. These matters are relevant, even essential, to the study of his poetry; but of supreme importance for the reader forty years after Owen's death is the quality of that poetry. That chance made Owen a war-poet is ultimately of less importance than the fact that he was a poet. The effect of the war on Owen's development and on his work cannot be ignored, but it is not the whole story. The remainder of this book will be concerned with that development in as wide a context as possible.

CHAPTER TWO

Owen's Early Ideas of Poetry

THE development traced in the last chapter shows more than the reflection in poetry of changes in the attitude towards war, for it indicates also a change in ideas on the nature and function of poetry itself and is thus directly relevant to the study of a young poet whose own ideas were undergoing a similar reappraisal at the same time. It helps to explain the paradox of his announcing ecstatically to his mother 'I am held peer by the Georgians' at the very time at which he was engaged upon the composition of poetry markedly different from and far more important than anything the Georgians produced. It throws light also on the celebrated statement in his draft Preface: 'Above all I am not concerned with Poetry', making it less enigmatic.

A fragmentary poem of Owen's begins with the lines

> The beautiful, the fair, the elegant,
> Is that which pleases us, says Kant,
> Without a thought of interest or advantage.

To object to the inadequacy of this as a statement of the Kantian critique may seem captious in its severity but it makes a convenient pointer to one of Owen's limitations, which it would be a disservice to him to conceal, so well does his later work overcome it. Owen was never in any sense of the phrase an 'intellectual poet'; to infer from this quotation that his acquaintance with Kant was unlikely to be closer than second-hand, even hearsay, is only to read it in the light of everything else we know about his education and reading. The passage suggests an affinity with the

aestheticism that sees beauty as an end in itself, capable of
separation from the 'thought of interest or advantage' and
presumably from normal considerations of morality. A good
deal of Owen's work confirms this impression of his in-
clinations, but this Kantian allusion would be misleading if
it were taken as implying any genuinely philosophical basis
for such a position. Owen's aestheticism was emotional and
derivative rather than the product of inner conviction and
it owes much more to his enthusiasm for Keats than to his
understanding of Kant. It is easy to censure it as immature
and escapist, but it played too large a part in his development to be lightly dismissed. The impression that Owen
became a poet solely as the result of meeting Siegfried
Sassoon at Craiglockhart is one that has gained some cur-
rency although Mr Sassoon would be the last person to wish
to see it perpetuated. The plain fact is that Owen had begun
writing poetry at a much earlier date and no study of his work
can afford to begin in 1917, however much it recognises the
indisputable inferiority of the greater part of the juvenilia.

The poetry of any young poet will bear unmistakable
traces of his reading and literary taste, and Owen was unusually impressionable and—certainly before 1917—young
even for his age. His debt to Keats which Edmund Blunden
illustrates so effectively in his memoir is not, therefore, surprising, but it must not obscure his susceptibility to other
influences as well. Like most young men of his generation
he had been brought up on popular nineteenth-century
Romantic poetry: from his poems and his letters it is clear
that he knew Shelley and Keats better than Wordsworth
and Coleridge, Tennyson better than Matthew Arnold. The
reference in a rhyming letter of 1911 to

> hills where Arnold wandered forth

Which, like his verse, still undulate in calm
And gentle beauty

betrays a somewhat one-sided view of Arnold's poetry
which is re-emphasised by a reading-list scribbled at a later,
though uncertain, date on the reverse of a draft poem; the
titles to which it refers—'Thyrsis', 'The Scholar Gipsy',
'Shakespeare', 'Lines written in Kensington Gardens' and
'The Forsaken Merman'—are all representative of the
'calm/And gentle beauty' that is conspicuously absent from
the tortured poems of doubt like 'Empedocles on Etna',
'Obermann Once More' or even 'Dover Beach'. The addition of the title *Literature and Dogma* does not radically correct the impression that Owen was much less familiar with
this other side of Arnold, especially since he originally—
though perhaps revealingly—wrote *Religion and Dogma* and
then corrected it. In short, it is emotional rather than philosophical Romanticism that attracted him and that accounts
also for his obvious delight in the poetry of Swinburne and
Wilde. He had read some Yeats, but it seems to have been
the Yeats of the Celtic twilight that impressed him rather
than the Yeats of *The Green Helmet* or *Responsibilities*; at
least the epigraphs of 'S.I.W.' and 'The Show' are taken
from *The King's Threshold* and the 1906 non-acting version
of *The Shadowy Waters* respectively. The rhyming letter
contains a fairly conventional reference to Gray and there
are indications elsewhere of a natural enjoyment of Shakespeare, but beyond this little can be said with confidence on
the subject of Owen's reading.

There is, for example, no evidence that he shared the
interest in seventeenth-century Metaphysical poetry which
the publication of H. J. C. Grierson's edition of Donne in
1912 had done so much to reawaken. That Isaac Rosenberg's

correspondence shows a familiarity with Donne and Cra-
shaw before 1914 not only confirms Owen's lesser intellectual curiosity but points also to a handicap under which
Owen laboured until 1917. Not only was Rosenberg three
years older than Owen but he had the added advantage of
being more closely in touch with other writers. From 1912
onwards Rosenberg was in regular correspondence with
Laurence Binyon, Gordon Bottomley, and Edward Marsh;
he had also in Miss Seaton an intelligent and stimulating
correspondent whose criticism he valued. Binyon's intro-
ductory memoir to the 1922 volume of Rosenberg's poems
contains a selection of his letters comparable in quantity
with Blunden's selection of Owen's but indicative of a range
of reading that included Jonson, Milton, Byron, Burns,
Rossetti, Pater, Emerson, and Whitman. Owen's reading
was probably more extensive than can be known, but it was
a reading much less critical than that of Rosenberg who had
more opportunity and the help of more experienced friends
to develop his critical judgment and his taste.

Owen was less fortunately placed. To be born in East
London, as Rosenberg was, may seem a doubtful blessing
but at least it gave him easier access to centres of culture than
did a boyhood spent in Oswestry and Shrewsbury. This
provincialism might have mattered less had there been, in
Owen's immediate circle, anyone well qualified either by
inclination or training to direct and guide the development
of a young poet. At all times interested in her son's poetic
aspirations, Mrs Owen undoubtedly encouraged them as
best she could, and it is to her that Owen wrote most regularly about his poetry and to her that his thoughts of home
most often turned. The part she played in preserving his
manuscripts and preparing for their publication, as well as
her energetic concern for his posthumous reputation, do her

a credit too great to be harmed by recognition of the fact that she was not sufficiently expert to be able to act as a whetstone for his critical judgments.

In 1912, while living with the vicar of the little Oxfordshire village of Dunsden, Owen attended some classes in botany at University College Reading (as it then was) and his tutor, discovering that he wrote poetry, sent him to her colleague, Edith Morley, in the Department of English. Miss Morley gave him an hour's tuition a week for some two terms and remembers reading some Ruskin with him, but the opportunity of literary companionship that this seemed to promote was cut prematurely short by the illness that necessitated his withdrawal from Reading. On his recovery he went as a tutor to Bordeaux in 1913 where, as will be seen later, his friendship with the poet Laurent Tailhade was of very considerable importance to his poetic development. If we exclude a brief and apparently inconclusive interview in 1915 with Harold Monro of the Poetry Bookshop, Tailhade was probably the only man of letters whose acquaintance Owen made before he met Sassoon.

His only other literary friendship of any consequence had been with a cousin of about his own age, E. Leslie Gunston, who lived near Reading and also wrote poetry. In friendly competition with his cousin and a young lady acquaintance, Owen used regularly to write poems on agreed topics and when in 1917 his cousin published a volume of lyrics (which he dedicated to Owen) at least five titles in its table of contents corresponded to titles of poems by Owen. For the rest of his life Owen remained on terms of intimacy with his cousin, sending him drafts of poems for comments, meeting him whenever possible on leave, and writing, until only a few days before his death, postcards and letters which in their easy informality and candour are significantly different from any of his correspondence that has been published; he also presented Sassoon with a copy of his cousin's poems, but doubtless without fully realising how closely that volume would have approximated to his own achievement had it not been for factors unforeseeable from his adolescence.

II

The loneliness, then, which forms a dominant motif in much of Owen's early poetry may be partly, as its conventionality of form and idiom imply, the product of a literary conviction that this is what poetry ought to be about, but it is the reflection also of a real, if not wholly conscious, sense of isolation on Owen's part. From the manuscripts this seems to have been particularly oppressive during his period at Dunsden, a period which he once described as characterised by 'bouts of religion'. One of the several incomplete poems that he scribbled on the backs of handbills advertising a missionary lantern lecture at Dunsden, envisages four stanzas expressing his sense of being cut off, at morn, noon, eve, and night consecutively, from the natural world and from all human experience except death. A sonnet of about the same time develops this sense of deprivation by contrasting the generosity of a rich landowner giving his parting guest a flower from his garden with the niggardliness of God in withholding from the poet any companionship; like so many of these unpublished pieces it is somewhat affected and selfconscious in its sensuous imagery and its mannered 'poetic' language, but its association of deprivation and religion is significant. Similarly, a number of these unpublished poems deal with unrequited love. One of these, the sonnet 'Autumnal', recalls the sestet of Rossetti's *Lovesight*; another sonnet, on the Sleeping Beauty theme,

37

despite an over-aureate octave, achieves a more individual note in its closing lines:

> For, when I kissed, her eyelids knew no stir
> So back I drew tiptoe from that Princess
> Because it was too soon, and not my part,
> To start voluptuous pulses in her heart,
> And kiss her to the world of Consciousness.

The moving shyness and immaturity of this is paralleled in the sonnet dated May 1916 which visualises Eros running hand-in-hand across a beach with two lovers, stopping short, and throwing them to the ground; it ends with the injunction

> mind that we
> Both laugh with love; and having tumbled, try
> To go forever children, hand in hand.
> The sea is rising . . . and the world is sand.

The lightness of touch here is more confidently sustained and it is a poem agreeably less derivative than many of the others but in its gaiety it is unquestionably a song of innocence rather than of experience.

To try to link such poems with relationships in Owen's personal experience is less relevant than to relate them to his published work. The theme of isolation finds its best treatment there in 'The Unreturning' where the idea of separation by death is employed to give it an intensity lacking in the other sonnets, and where a much less hackneyed imagery used with discrimination and feeling suggests poetic depths unsuspected in them. Rupert Brooke's approach to a similar theme in his sonnet 'Failure' makes an interesting comparison, especially in its sestet:

> All the great courts were quiet in the sun,
>   And full of vacant echoes: most had grown

> Over the glassy pavements, and begun
>> To creep within the dusty council-halls.
> An idle wind blew round an empty throne
>> And stirred the heavy curtains on the walls.

Both reject in youthful disillusion the conventional idea of heaven and are oppressed by the emptiness they are obliged to substitute for it. Brooke's heaven is more sharply visualised, Owen's more deeply felt. There is a hard, clear light suffusing Brooke's scene, where Owen deliberately builds up an indeterminate impression of mistiness. Brooke's 'vacant echoes' are hollow, empty, and reverberating; Owen's 'vacant gloaming', by its association with a dawn that 'peers', the sadness of 'half-lit minds', and 'sick men's sighs', becomes haunted and therefore haunting. Brooke's certainty of the emptiness of his heaven, with its vacated throne, produces a sonnet technically accomplished but cold, and much closer to some of the unpublished sonnets of Owen's just discussed, than to 'The Unreturning' which in spirit resembles more nearly Walter de la Mare in such poems as 'The Listeners'. The dead whom Owen cannot bring back in this poem are none the less felt presences: they are what he was on another occasion to call 'The Kind Ghosts', and they become the 'encumbered sleepers' of whom one was later, in 'Strange Meeting', to establish communication with the poet who here feels himself so cut off from them. (Such a connection between the two poems may find conjectural support from Owen's inclusion in his draft Table of Contents, under the heading 'Doubtful', of the title 'A ponderous day'; that one version of 'The Unreturning' began with the phrase 'A ponderous night' suggests that the poem he had in mind (otherwise unidentifiable with any known to me) was this one, imperfectly recollected.)

The ghost as an expression of the poet's loneliness recurs in 'Shadwell Stair', a beautifully realised little poem with something of the evocative quality of a Whistler Nocturne. Owen's use of the 'In Memoriam' metre here is appropriate to what is in effect a 'mood poem', but it is sufficiently individualised not to appear derivative. The final line of this poem links it clearly with the other aspect of loneliness already noted in the unpublished pieces, the loneliness of the frustrated lover, which forms the theme of an interesting group of accomplished, if occasionally obscure, sonnets in the published volume.

Of these the most straightforward is 'To Eros', where again the Georgian affinities are clearly marked in the structure, the diction, and the attempt at boldness in the bridegroom image, as well as in the whole theme of Romanticised disillusion. The three closing lines are of a quality indisputably higher than that of many of these earlier poems, but there is still the suggestion of an exercise about the whole poem; as in many of Brooke's carefully-wrought sonnets there is a hint of technique outrunning experience, just as there is in the delightful and more original 'From My Diary, July 1914'. A more complex poem that still does not wholly escape a similar criticism is 'My Shy Hand', although an unpublished version (dated 29–30 August 1917) seems preferable to the printed one for its avoidance of the affected archaisms 'hath' and 'sleepeth' and of the second person singular constructions which are used consistently except in the penultimate line. There are five manuscript versions of this sonnet, three of which —including the one already mentioned—use the second person pronoun where the printed poem uses the first and vice versa; that is, the poem appears to have been first conceived as an address to a woman or, as the title of one states, 'to Beauty'. The 'speaker' in 'My

Shy Hand', then (and the title is Blunden's) may most satis-
factorily be visualised as a goddess, Aphrodite, in the familiar
attitude with one hand on her breast; if so, the consciously
elevated diction of this version may have been intended to
enhance the dignity of the goddess. This and the Tennysonian quality of the poetry (as distinct from the imagery)
make it a young man's poem about Love rather than a love
poem in the more usual sense; its delight in

> Languor of June all winterlong, and ease
> For ever from the vain untravelled leagues

connects it with the enervating atmosphere of 'The Lotos-
Eaters' rather than with the exploratory energy of 'Ulysses',
but despite such hints of immaturity of outlook Owen's
growing mastery of the sonnet form is clearly asserting itself.

The 'storm' from which the penultimate line promises to
shelter the poet had, in the previous October, itself been the
subject of a very powerful sonnet remarkable for the range
of its associational reference. The 'he' of 'Storm' may, as
in the other sonnet, be Eros and the theme, like that of the
sleeping beauty sonnet and 'Music' which was composed at
about the same time as 'Storm', may again be the awakening
of love but this time more tragically conceived. (In another
unpublished sonnet, entitled 'The Peril of Love', Owen
says he has "found too late love's grave significance".) It
may be a symbolic statement of apprehension for his personal future, the 'he' being a personification of war, although the insistence on 'his' beauty makes this less likely.
Alternatively Owen may be visualising his poetic career as
an attempt to win fame from Apollo which is doomed to
glorious failure ('I quite envisage possibility of non-success'
he had written in March 1915, and a similar idea recurs in
the 'Identity Disc' sonnet, while the unpublished sonnet just

quoted speaks of 'love's grave significance' as 'far above/The zeal for fame or fortune'); or it may be nothing more personal than an experimental variation on the theme of Hyperion, but whichever interpretation is favoured, the way in which the image of the lightning-struck tree is developed and sustained throughout the sonnet shows an intensity of poetic skill more mature than that in any other poem so far discussed.

This anticipation of the quality of his best work is a reminder that by the time this sonnet was written Owen was on the brink of the great creative phase of his life with which the remainder of this book will be concerned, but this did not mean a conscious abandoning of the themes of these earlier poems, nor was the decadent-Romantic impetus behind the juvenilia wholly exorcised. His bracketing of his own name with the Georgians occurs only ten months before his death. Among the manuscripts that he sent to Osbert Sitwell, as late as the summer of 1918, he included a piece dated four years earlier which is remarkable for the inferiority of its Swinburnian pastiche, and several other unpublished drafts on which he was working at Scarborough in 1918 also indicate the survival of this impulse towards a lush aestheticism. For all these reasons it will be well to summarise a few conclusions on this aspect of his work before proceeding, and the pastiche just referred to will provide a convenient method of doing this.

III

Comprising twenty-five lines of undistinguished blank verse in spelling unusually erratic even for the young Owen, this poem is an invocation to an unspecified deity whose associations with passion, blood, and violent death prompt in the poet a frenzied exultation at this fusion of beauty and sin. Such, at least, seems to have been the intention, but the real motivation behind the poem seems to have been only a surfeit of Swinburne and Wilde, as is apparent from the heavily-accented alliteration, the reliance on a naïvely-employed sensuous imagery that recalls Wilde's 'The Sphinx', and such phrases as 'furious beauty', 'wild desire', and 'bitter pleasure'. There is more than a little adolescent bravado about the rhetorical flourishing of this decadence, and its paganism seems forced, self-conscious, and literary. Owen's cousin recalls their reading Swinburne together 'by the hour' and some of the poems in his own volume reflect this influence. A similar note recurs in Owen's unpublished sonnet 'Purple' (one of the pieces that he began in com-petition with his cousin and was still revising in 1917) which is also reminiscent of Brooke's South Seas poems. Never-theless, the attitude underlying 'Long Ages Past' is not wholly affectation, for it recurs throughout the juvenilia with deepening significance. That Owen should have felt religion to be at variance with poetry is less surprising than it is regrettable, for it seems to have led him into an artificial and initially constricting dichotomy which necessitated the subordination of one complete side of his personality when writing poetry. Had he had the strength of will and intellect to resolve that dichotomy, or at least to commit himself more wholly either to aestheticism or to Christianity, his early poetry would have gained considerably. As it is, T. E. Hulme's celebrated observation that 'Romanticism is spilt religion' has a literalness of application to Owen, for in these poems the consistently attempted divorce between art and belief bespeaks a genuinely religious nature temporarily at a loss. Thus an unpublished sonnet 'Maundy Thursday' (dated 1916), after describing the varying significance of a crucifix to different worshippers, ends:

Then I too knelt before that acolyte.
Above the crucifix I bent my head:
The Christ was thin, and cold, and very dead:
And yet I bowed, yea, kissed—my lips did cling
(I kissed the warm live hand that held the thing).

Unpolished as these lines are, they are important not only
for their independence and forthrightness but also as the first
explicit treatment of a theme that becomes increasingly
prominent later. Another passage of unpublished blank
verse, even more markedly sensuous, apotheosises the Flesh
as a 'strange regnant Presence' re-creating the world until
its own crucifixion is called for; the poem is too incomplete
to represent a satisfactory synthesis and like other passages
in poems and letters suggests a nascent aestheticism at that
point of development not wholly integrated either with
poetry or with personality.

Among the published poems this cult of beauty achieves
its best expression in 'The Fates', of which sonnet Owen
sent his cousin a transcript on 1 July 1917 describing it as
embodying 'an Idea—which is almost my Gospel'. That
such a gospel was not unique to Owen may most easily be
seen by comparing a sonnet of Masefield's entitled 'Forget',
especially its sestet:

And I, O Beauty, O divine white wonder,
On whom my dull eyes, blind to all else, peer,
Have you for peace, that not the whole war's thunder,
Nor the world's wreck, can threat or take from here.
So you remain, though all man's passionate seas
Roar their blind tides. I can forget all these.

There is no question of plagiarism here for Masefield's
sonnet was not published until 1919 and Owen's not until
1931; the obvious similarities of tone and idiom may thus

be ascribed to the fact that both poets clearly have in mind the sonnets of Shakespeare which, consciously or not, they are imitating. Similarly Owen's 'Identity Disc' sonnet is recognisably Shakespearian in form and inspiration, even without the corroborative evidence of one manuscript of it on the reverse of which he has transcribed from memory Shakespeare's 'To me, fair friend, you never can be old'.

The parallel with Masefield establishes the Georgianism of Owen's aestheticism just as surely as do the parallels with Brooke referred to above, or the similarity between the sultry exoticism of 'Long Ages Past' and that of Flecker's *Hassan*: all of them are drawing, not on each other, but on common sources, and with a common desire to escape from the pressing actualities of their time. Owen alone among them realised the ultimate impossibility of this. In 'The Fates' beauty was to be the solution to a personal problem of growing old:

> So I'll evade the vice and rack of age
> And miss the march of lifetime, stage by stage.

In 'Strange Meeting' the dead enemy claims to have derived from his earlier aestheticism the power

> To miss the march of this retreating world

(the repetition of phrase is revealing), but it is a power that he would have exercised only temporarily and in the interests of humanity, not of himself. It is in that poem that Owen comes nearest to the synthesis between religion and the cult of beauty that he was incapable of earlier, and for him as for the protagonist of 'Strange Meeting' it was his experience of war that gave him this insight.

War did not destroy Owen's idea of beauty but it widened it immeasurably, as is apparent not only from 'Apologia

45

pro Poemate Meo' but also from the fragmentary poem
'Beauty' referred to at the beginning of this chapter. It
includes these lines, the almost cynical realism of which is
markedly different from 'The Fates':

> Men seldom speak of beauty, beauty as such,
> Not even lovers think about it much.
> Women of course consider it for hours
> In mirrors

but the real point of this poem comes in the continuation of
it which Blunden transcribes separately in his manuscript
notebook but apparently does not connect with the fragment he prints. Owen has not fully worked out the con-
necting links between the two passages but their relationship
is marked by the repetition of the Kant quotation, this time
in ironical key, for the continuation appears to record the
only instance that occurs to Owen of men speaking of
beauty. A soldier swimming sustains a shrapnel wound,
prompting the immediate cry from his companions 'What
a beauty!' much in the spirit of one of Owen's letters of
April 1917:

> Another night I was putting out an advanced post when we
> were seen or heard and greeted with shrapnel. The man
> crouching shoulder to shoulder to me gets a beautiful round
> hole pierced deep in his biceps. I am nothing so fortunate,
> being only buffeted in the eyes by the shock and whacked on
> the calf by a spent fragment which scarcely tore the puttee.

Like 'The Chances' and 'S.I.W.' this indicates the soldier's
attitude to the slight flesh wound which is just serious
enough to qualify as a 'Blighty one' and thus ensure the
wounded man a return to England, but not serious enough
to incapacitate him: it is only thus that they can conceive

of beauty. By a final grim irony the poem was apparently to have ended with the 'beauty' turning gangrenous and the soldier being buried at sea on the passage home. This fragmentary poem would have needed much revision and working over, as well as completion, but enough of it survives to form an interesting example of Owen's development: the connection between beauty and death which is here ironically brought out is altogether more meaningful, more convincing, and more mature than the conventional decadence of the juvenilia.

If Owen's remark 'Above all, I am not concerned with Poetry' rests on the assumption that the proper themes of poetry are loneliness, love, and beauty, and if he would have been surprised to discover posterity attaching greater importance to his war poetry than to his more conventional lyrics, his assumption is not necessarily erroneous. What he perhaps overlooked is the way in which war was to modify these themes so that even his own war poetry may still be said to deal with them. Loneliness becomes the splendid detachment that makes possible such poems as 'The Show' and 'Mental Cases'; love, which had seemed so disappointing in 'To Eros', was to become 'Greater Love', and in its fusion with pity was to find and record in these great poems the tragic beauty of human suffering.

CHAPTER THREE

The Impact of the War on Owen's Poetry

THE 'innately gentle artist' we have so far considered would have assented unhesitatingly to Matthew Arnold's dictum 'no one can deny that it is of advantage to a poet to deal with a beautiful world', and when the beautiful world of his youthful imaginings was unceremoniously replaced by a world even more harsh, sordid and repulsive than 'Burn's world of Scotch drink, Scotch religion, and Scotch manners' that had prompted Arnold's original reflection, Owen had either to make some adjustment or capitulate entirely to those new pressures. It seems unlikely that Owen ever entertained the innocently heroic expectations with which Henry Fleming in *The Red Badge of Courage* enlisted, but in its sharpness and horror the impact war made on him is not unlike the effect it had on Stephen Crane's young man whose first reaction was one of embittered anger:

> The youth turned, with sudden, livid rage, toward the battle-field. He shook his fist. He seemed about to deliver a philippic.

The main difference is that Owen's poetic fist was waved not so much at the battlefield as in another direction, but there is something of the philippic about what were probably his first completed poems of war experience, 'Dulce et Decorum Est' and 'The Dead-Beat'. (I except 'Exposure' because there seems good reason to believe that it was considerably revised at a date later than the February 1917 to which it has hitherto been assigned.) Both of these poems definitely belong to August 1917, when Owen had been invalided home after his first spell of trench warfare, and thus

to the first month of his personal acquaintance at Craiglockhart with Siegfried Sassoon, whose poems he already knew
and admired.

One obvious way in which a young poet might protest
against the ugliness of this war-world would be to contrast
it directly with the beauty it is destroying, and that this
indeed is the prescription that 'Dulce et Decorum Est' was
first intended to follow may be seen from the version
printed in the Notes to the standard edition; here the vividly
repulsive picture of the gas casualty is interrupted by an ex-
hortation to the 'certain poetess' who is being apostro-
phised to

> think how once his face was like a bud,
> Fresh as a country rose, and keen, and young,

—a conventionally beautiful image which appears to have
struck Owen, on reconsideration, as too expansive, romantic, and sentimental in its context, for it is very firmly cancelled in the next draft. An even more extreme instance of
this tendency occurs in a draft of 'Mental Cases' where the
bowed heads of the shell-shocked are likened to foxgloves—

> Aloof, lone foxgloves in their ferny glooms—

in an image, developed over three lines, that in any of his
earlier poems would have been delightful but that is quite
inappropriate here. Drafts of several poems, especially 'Anthem for Doomed Youth', show how easily Owen slipped
into a hackneyed Romantic idiom of grandiloquent and lush
imagery, and one sees why, in *Siegfried's Journey*, Sassoon
recalls himself

> censuring the over-luscious writing in his immature pieces. . . .
> But it was the emotional element, even more than its verbal
> expression, which seemed to need refinement. There was an

almost embarrassing sweetness in the sentiment of some of his work, though it showed skill in rich and melodious combinations of words.

Whether it was Sassoon's censure, his own innate poetic tact, or a combination of both is uncertain, but his cancellation of the 'country rose' image in 'Dulce et Decorum Est' was followed by a desire to heighten the impression of ugliness still further. He accordingly began on an interlinear insertion which is of interest in itself and which has also had a curious history.

Apparently, when he had inserted the first phrase, he realised that there was insufficient space for his purpose and he therefore completed the emendation at the foot of the page, beginning half-way across the sheet with the words 'bitter as the cud' and continuing down to 'to children'. In spite of the absence of any indication both editors recognised the place of these lines in the body of the poem (though the 1920 edition reads 'Bitten') but neither appears to have noticed the three words pencilled in interlineally. These obviously belong to the same revision as the lines at the foot; by their position and initial capital they are clearly the first half of a line of which the second half (by its indentation and lower-case 'b' in 'bitter') follows at the end of the text. There seems, in fact, no doubt that Owen intended not the half-line as printed but a full line, reading 'Obscene as cancer, bitter as the cud', the idea of cancer coming perhaps from the original rose image by the intermediate association of 'canker'. The promptness and sureness with which Owen expunged or modified these purple patches, here and on other occasions, make Yeats' gibe—'He is all blood, dirt, and sucked sugar-stick'—unfair in its severity.

That another way of eliminating this sweetness had already presented itself to Owen may be seen from the other poem written in August 1917, 'The Dead-Beat'. An early draft of this he sent to his cousin on the 22nd, describing it as 'in Sassoon's style' and as being written 'after leaving him', but a marginal note on the manuscript itself draws attention to something less self-evident: against a version of the doctor's comment that differs slightly in wording, though not in sentiment from the lines as published, Owen has written 'Those are the very words!' Thus both 'The Dead-Beat' and 'Dulce et Decorum Est' serve as a convenient index to the immediate impact that the war had on his poetry. The more conventional 'poetic' attitudes of his earlier self-expression, real as they may have seemed to him at the time, are giving way to a more urgent communication, a report on experience, that relies for its authenticity on 'the very words', the bare bones of the experience presented without what he was later to call 'poets' tearful fooling'. Part of Owen's greatness as a poet lies in the integrity with which he subordinates his predilections for a beautiful world to his sense of realism in his poems of war, for it is from this self-discipline that his best poetry springs, and one of the ironies of his sudden death is that it becomes the means whereby the dedicated thoroughness of that self-discipline is revealed.

'Most writers,' said Johnson, 'by publishing their own works, prevent all various readings, and preclude all conjectural criticism.' Death on active service in 1918 deprived Wilfred Owen of this privilege, of which most modern poets have availed themselves freely by suppressing or modifying earlier work in later editions. In his own lifetime he published only four poems, of which at least two are not among his best: 'Song of Songs' appeared in *The Hydra*, the magazine of Craiglockhart Military Hospital, on 1 September 1917, 'Miners' in *The Nation*, 16 January 1918, and

'Futility' and 'Hospital Barge at Cérisy' in *The Nation*, 15 June 1918. After his death his manuscripts passed into the hands of his mother who acted as his literary executor and who, in accordance with his wishes, destroyed some but preserved the remainder intact, making them available to Siegfried Sassoon and Edith Sitwell, who prepared the first selection of Owen's poems to be published in book form in 1920, and later to Edmund Blunden, whose larger, more critical edition appeared in 1931, has since been frequently reprinted in this country and in the U.S., and remains the standard text. Many, although not all, of these manuscripts later passed into the possession of the British Museum; their range gives a most informative picture of Owen's evolution as a poet during the whole of his short lifetime, and the existence of sometimes as many as six variant transcripts of the same poem throws light on the genesis and growth of individual poems. Of 'Anthem for Doomed Youth', for example, there are four manuscripts in the British Museum and a fifth in private ownership; internal evidence, as well as notes on two of them by Owen and Sassoon, facilitates their arrangement in chronological order, and the study of the many emendations and tentative experiments by which the final form was reached is a fascinating and rewarding task. This aspect of the manuscripts, as well as some textual emendations that they appear to warrant, will be developed in Chapter Seven: my present purpose is to refer to two ways in which they illuminate Owen's intentions in his war poems and show what he hoped those poems would achieve.

II

When, probably in the last months of his life, Owen planned to publish a volume of poems he drafted a Preface which should have made clear his intentions beyond doubt.

Unfortunately, it was not only never completed but it survives in only one manuscript, heavily corrected and in places wellnigh indecipherable, so that the editors of the two editions differ radically in their readings of it. One crucial passage is reprinted in the 1920 edition in the form 'Yet these elegies are not to this generation. This is in no sense consolatory. They may be to the next'. This implies a recognition on Owen's part of the prophetic nature of his poems, which are addressed not to his own unsympathetic generation but to a later one who will find his attitude to war more acceptable. C. Day Lewis in *A Hope for Poetry* (1934) quotes the passage in this form and draws this inference from it, with the added authority of Owen's growing reputation. Blunden, however, prints 'Yet these elegies are to this generation in no sense consolatory. They may be to the next'. Here the implication is that the poems *are* addressed to Owen's generation but not as consolation; they are not, that is, the 'bardic' type of war poems which exalt, encourage, and thus console, the reader, but a challenge, calculated, by their relentless exposure of the pity of war, to disturb the equanimity and indifference into which the reader has been lulled by a surfeit of pseudo-hortatory verse. To a later generation they may be consolatory, presumably as the picture of a barbaric past now over. The first reading is perhaps more flattering to Owen's prophetic powers, the second more in accord with the Owen who on leave carried a set of photographs of trench casualties with which to bring home the reality of war to the arm-chair warriors.

In fact, the manuscript leaves no room for doubt. The crucial sentence has been drastically revised in structure but the emendations show no change in its meaning; careful reconstruction of the successive steps by which it was changed is possible and establishes the rightness of Blunden's version. In order to obtain the earlier reading a number of interlinear corrections have to be interpreted, with considerable latitude, as a line of consecutive prose, and some cancellations have arbitrarily to be ignored while others are retained. That Owen thought of these poems primarily as propaganda is clear not only from the tenor of the whole Preface but also from his Table of Contents (some other implications of which will be discussed later) where the notes under the heading 'Motive' show exactly the manner in which each poem was intended to further the central object of inspiring loathing for the bestialities of war. The sentence 'Above all I am not concerned with Poetry' indicates, especially by its upper-case initial in 'Poetry', an emphatic distinction between what he wanted to write and what the urgency of the occasion demanded; at the same time, he had originally written 'That is why the true War Poets must be truthful', and the universalisation of the principle which the deletion of 'War' effects constitutes perhaps a tacit recognition of the dangers of too categorical a distinction.

The much-quoted statement 'The Poetry is in the pity' necessitates reference at this stage to two other manuscripts which authorise the only major emendation needing to be made to the published canon. Blunden prints without comment two poems, 'The Calls' (p. 97) and 'And I must go' (p. 100), neither of which seems complete in itself but both of which make a great deal more sense if read consecutively as one poem. (A transcript in private ownership suggests that two other fragments, 'Has your soul sipped?' (p. 28) and 'It is not death' (p. 56) may, with some unpublished stanzas, constitute one poem, but this is not so capable of definite proof). Only one manuscript of each poem exists; 'The Calls' as printed occupies the whole of one sheet, and the stanzas beginning 'Gongs hum and buzz' are on a separate sheet untitled, 'And I must go' being supplied by Blunden. The two sheets are of identical paper (a fact which cannot be ignored in view of the great variety of paper Owen uses, from notepaper to restaurant bills, the backs of missionary lantern-lecture advertisements, and the dust-jacket of an edition of Keats) and the calligraphy (which also varies extensively) is consistent as well. The stanza form of the two printed pieces differs, 'The Calls' having three rhyming decasyllabic lines and a fourth of varying length rhyming internally, while the other is irregular. This is due to the incompleteness of the draft; the first two stanzas on the second sheet show an abandoned attempt at a fourth line of the same pattern as 'The Calls' and the last stanza. Further corroboration of their connection is provided by an abandoned title on the first sheet, 'From my Window', which clearly refers more directly to the last two stanzas of the second sheet than to the first. The most conclusive proof, of course, lies in the logical development of thought which they exhibit. Owen is considering in turn various possible poetic themes. Labour, childhood and education, religion, military training, even the 'black market', fail in turn to arouse any response in him; he is impervious to everything except the human suffering evoked in the last two stanzas. In the manuscript the point receives additional emphasis in the last line which ends 'And *this time* I must go' (I italicise the words omitted by Blunden). There is also a progressive time sequence in all seven stanzas, a structure paralleled in the earlier unpublished poem referred to at p. 37 above. The punctuation in the third stanza also needs correction: two apostrophes in the manuscript (religion's and pigeons') clarify the meaning, 'amen' being understood after each possessive.

Though more satisfactory than either of its two consti-
tuent fragments, this seven-stanza poem would have needed
some revision to have eradicated the hint of glibness from
its metre and there are amusing signs of the difficulty Owen
was having with the internally-rhyming fourth lines of the
incomplete stanzas. Neverless it is important for the simple
directness of its final stanza:

> For leaning out last midnight on my sill
> I heard the sighs of men, that have no skill
> To speak of their distress, no, nor the will!
> A voice I know. And this time I must go.

In its context this becomes a fine poetic counterpart to the
prose declaration to his mother:

> I came out in order to help these boys—directly by leading
> them as well as an officer can, indirectly by watching their
> sufferings that I may speak of them as well as a pleader can.

The extent to which pity had taken his poetry beyond
philippic and protest may be epitomised by relating 'The
Calls' to the letter of July 1918 in which he announces his
drafting oversea: the parallel between the two is so close
that the final stanza may well be a literal allusion to that
posting. That the poem was composed at Scarborough,
while Owen was with the Reserve Battalion, is implied by
collocation of references to everyday civilian life as well as
to infantry training and gunnery practice just as surely as by
the identification of the 'food-hog' whetting 'his gold-
filled tusk' in stanza 5 with 'all the stinking Leeds and Bradford war-profiteers now reading *John Bull* on Scarborough
sands' to whom the letter refers; that these cloth-manufac-
turers, who had made fortunes from providing the Government with military uniforms at inflated prices, were a

familiar symbol of profiteering may be seen not only from their reappearance in the Scarborough setting in Osbert Sitwell's *Before the Bombardment* but also from the allusion to 'the Bradford millionaire' at line 234 of *The Waste Land*. The whole tone of Owen's letter carries so irresistible a suggestion of Sassoon's 'Blighters' as to add emphasis to the weary refusal of 'The Calls' to rise even to the opportunity of poetic satire that the subject affords.

One reason for this may be found in the poem itself, if the unexpected phrase 'my *small* heart thumps' (my italics) is related to his use of a similar image on two other occasions. In 'Insensibility' it is applied to those 'who lose imagination':

> And terror's first constriction over,
> Their hearts remain small-drawn.

'Greater Love' refers to a heart which was

> never hot,
> Nor large, nor full like hearts made great with shot.

The experience of war, then, may enlarge or constrict the heart: in 'The Calls' Owen, by the implication that his is congenitally small, distinguishes himself from those who have suffered more from war experience than he. Not only does the line effectively suggest the insignificance of the human figure at the window against the larger world of gunnery and night but, more important, it communicates an affecting humility which recalls 'Apologia pro Poemate Meo' much more than 'Dulce et Decorum Est' or 'The Dead-Beat'. Humility is not the spirit which generates either the philippic or the satire, both of which require a confidence of superiority. Protest has given way to pleading for the inarticulate; indignation has turned to pity and to a mature sense of responsibility for others, rather than superiority to them, as may be seen by comparing 'Dulce et Decorum Est' with 'The Sentry'.

Both are poems of dramatic description that seek to make more vivid to the reader the physical and psychological suffering of war in terms of an eye-witness account of how one man became a casualty. The desire to communicate the immediacy of sharply-apprehended sensations finds onomatopoeic expression in

And thud! flump! thud! down the steep steps came thumping
And splashing in the flood, deluging muck,
The sentry's body.

A draft of the earlier poem had tried to suggest the fall of gas-shells by 'Whew . . . fup, fop, fup', and an abandoned draft of 'The Sentry' had contained the line 'Suddenly a whizzbang boxed our ears'. If the omission of that line from the final version is something of a pity, it does draw attention to the more primarily visual emphasis in both these poems: both rely on a nightmare use of under-water imagery

But someone still was yelling out and stumbling
And floundering like a man in fire or lime.
Dim through the misty panes and thick green light,
As under a green sea, I saw him drowning.
In all my dreams before my helpless sight
He plunges at me, guttering, choking, drowning.

'The Sentry' involves the narrator in the predicament more directly:

Eyeballs, huge-bulged like squids',
Watch my dreams still; but I forgot him there
In posting next for duty, and sending a scout
To beg a stretcher somewhere, and floundering about
To other posts under the shrieking air.

In his forgetting of the casualty he may seem less emotionally affected than in 'Dulce et Decorum Est', but this time he is not watching someone's suffering from behind the immunity of a gas-mask or a dream but himself 'floundering' (the recurrence of the verb is significant) like the casualties as unnaturally in war as in another element. After the opening paragraph 'Dulce et Decorum Est' focuses exclusively, in the manner of the cinema close-up, on the individual agony while simultaneously insisting on the impossibility of the spectator's conceiving it:

> If in some smothering dreams, you too could pace
> Behind the wagon that we flung him in,
> And watch the white eyes writhing in his face,
> His hanging face, like a devil's sick of sin;
> If you could hear, at every jolt, the blood
> Come gargling from the froth-corrupted lungs,
> Obscene as cancer, bitter as the cud
> Of vile, incurable sores on innocent tongues . . .

The more hyperbolical the accumulation of detail, the more we resist it as 'propaganda' in the pejorative sense, but in 'The Sentry' the focus is changed, the wounded sentry is forgotten in the hurry of the emergency and in the general welter of affliction; instead of the catalogue of horror there is the even more effective shrinking from it in understatement:

> Those other wretches, how they bled and spewed,
> And one who would have drowned himself for good,
> I try not to remember these things now.
> Let dread hark back for one word only. . . .

and that 'one word' is also descriptive, not the moralising comment that ends 'Dulce et Decorum Est'. Moreover, where that poem deals exclusively with the physical pain of the gassed man 'The Sentry' widens the perspective to include not only the fear and pathetic self-delusion of the blinded youth as well as the suffering of his companions, but even a new dimension of time in the past suffering that still haunts the dug-out:

> What murk of air remained stank old, and sour
> With fumes of whizz-bangs, and the smell of men
> Who'd lived there years, and left their curse in the den,
> If not their corpses. . . .

The addition of smell to the sensory range of the poem is also indicative of the extension of Owen's powers since 'Dulce et Decorum Est', but the main difference between the two poems is that where the earlier is the immediate product of the white-hot indignation to which he had been brought (as one manuscript reveals) by the patriotic lines of Miss Jessie Pope that frequently graced the popular newspapers, 'The Sentry' is a report on experience in a much richer sense, muted yet imaginatively evocative where the other is strident and exhausting.

III

The type of poetry, then, to which Owen's conscience impelled him is a peculiarly difficult kind to write. The product of strongly held convictions, when the motivating feelings are most intense it is likely to become cheaply rhetorical as did so much minor but unquestionably sincere left-wing poetry in the 1930's; the outcome of a deeply-felt pity for the suffering of others, it has somehow to avoid the double pitfall of telling the reader about the pity, for that would become sentimentality, and of over-emphasising the suffering, for that would become painful morbidity. Certainly there is this much justification for Yeats's rejection from *The Oxford Book of Modern Verse* of 'certain poems written in the midst of the great war . . . for the same reason that made Arnold withdraw his *Empedocles on Etna* from circulation; passive suffering is not a theme for poetry'. While admitting that in pleading the suffering of others Owen makes that suffering his own, Yeats does not, as with justification he might have done, invoke one of his own most perceptive distinctions: 'We make out of the quarrel with others rhetoric but out of the quarrel with ourselves poetry.' Owen's work does become rhetorical when he is quarrelling with others—with Jessie Pope in 'Dulce et Decorum Est', with the clergy in 'At a Calvary near the Ancre', with the older generation in 'The Parable of the Old Men and the Young'; the satiric ferocity that Sassoon brought to bear on these subjects in, respectively, 'Blighters', 'They', and 'On Reading the War Diary of a Defunct Ambassador' gives the quarrel a bias that Owen (except in 'Smile, Smile, Smile') did not want. It cannot be claimed for Owen that he was invariably successful in avoiding the morbid and the sentimental, but the extent to which he does avoid them may not unreasonably be also attributed to the quarrel with himself out of which sprang so much of his best poetry.

CHAPTER FOUR

Elegies to this Generation

To see some of the ways in which Owen makes poetry out of the quarrel with himself we may conveniently start with 'Inspection' which, by its very structure, immediately illustrates the dilemma of a poet who is 'not concerned with poetry'. The first eight lines are dramatically factual in a convincingly colloquial manner; the second half uses a heightened poetic idiom (in something of the way in which, in 'S.I.W.', 'The Poem' is separated from 'The Action') for commentary and as a vehicle for the coherent expression of ideas which the character could not, in actuality, have formulated nearly so articulately. Yet the poem's unity is maintained not only by its continuity of dramatic scene as well as its theme but also by the skilful placing of a literary allusion which eases the transition and strikes the keynote of the poem. The young soldier, who has been punished for being dirty on parade,

> told me afterwards, the damned spot
> Was blood, his own. "Well, blood is dirt," I said.

'The damned spot' deliberately recalls the occasion of Lady Macbeth's sleepwalking when blood was indeed dirt—the irremovable dirt of guilt—and the association is sustained a few lines later by the reference to the washing out of stains, but the same image also carries a sacrificial overtone ('Are you washed in the Blood of the Lamb?') which anticipates the grim irony of the final lines:

> But when we're duly white-washed, being dead,
> The race will bear Field-Marshal God's inspection.

This reversion to the vernacular contributes to the unity of the poem, but equally important is its sardonic suggestion of the military ritual that survives even in war-time of 'white-washing' a camp before a G.O.C.'s inspection—a process so familiar to the soldier that he has his own terse but expressive synonym for it. What the inspecting officer sees—and is presumably gratified to see—is not the living reality of the camp but the camp in an artificial state of, to use Milton's phrase, 'excremental whiteness' from which the vitality has been drained off in the interest of outward show and dull conformity. This is a poem about guilt, but not the guilt of the young soldier so much as of a hypocritical world that is trying vicariously to expiate its own sins by the sacrifice of its youth ('Young blood's its great objection'). The process, however, is not purgative but negative, for the washing out of stains washes out the life as well. Another 'Parable of the Old Men and the Young', 'Inspection' becomes less of an overt quarrel with others than the 'Parable' by the irony of its situation which makes the young soldier the odd man out. Not only does the inspecting Deity this time want the sacrifice which in the other poem he rejected, but here Owen, in his primary dramatic role of an officer carrying out his duty, tacitly assumes a share in this universal guilt which, in his secondary role as poet, he is exposing.

The divided responsibility dramatised here causes the quarrel with himself out of which he makes poetry, as the dualism of the blood imagery here and elsewhere conveniently illustrates. Blood is a symbol of guilt, so that, for his 'Mental Cases', oppressed by the guilt of the 'multitudinous murders they once witnessed', blood has become obsessive:

> Sunlight seems a blood-smear; night comes blood-black;
> Dawn breaks open like a wound that bleeds afresh.

The dramatic emphasis of this poem, as of 'Inspection' and 'The Show', is on the incrimination of others, of the readers and of the poet who are mercilessly indicted in its closing lines, for the blood of these men is on their hands. Throughout his poetry blood is painful not merely because of its association with pain and suffering but painful in the vividness of its representation. In 'Insensibility' he half envies those 'who lose imagination', because

> Having seen all things red
> Their eyes are rid
> Of the hurt of the colour of blood for ever

but he has no intention of allowing his readers the luxury of this insensibility. The ubiquity of blood in the 'crimson slaughter' of war is insisted upon time and again in pictorial imagery of striking intensity, but seldom in an exclusively sensational way. The shell-shocked soldiers of 'Mental Cases' see all nature in terms of blood, but it is more usual for his poetry to present blood in terms of nature. Thus, in 'Asleep',

> And soon the slow, stray blood came creeping
> From the intrusive lead, like ants on track;

in 'Spring Offensive',

> earth set sudden cups
> In thousands for their blood

and in 'The Kind Ghosts',

> Not marvelling why her roses never fall
> Nor what red mouths were torn to make their blooms.

A pointer to the significance of this may again be found in 'Inspection' where to the young soldier the association of blood and dirt takes his thought

> Far off to where his wound had bled
> And almost merged for ever into clay.

To complain, as Yeats did, that Owen is 'all blood and dirt' is not only to ignore the prominence of those elements in the world of which Owen wrote but also to underestimate the genius with which his poetry fuses them symbolically and invests them with a life-giving significance.

Blood merging with clay or, as he puts it in 'Disabled', being poured 'down shell-holes till the veins ran dry', had become so familiar to the serving soldier that Owen allows his crippled spokesman in 'A Terre' to dilate upon it with philosophic humour:

> "I shall be one with nature, herb, and stone,"
> Shelley would tell me. Shelley would be stunned:
> The dullest Tommy hugs that fancy now.
> "Pushing up daisies" is their creed, you know.

Nothing was more characteristic of the vast battlefield of the Western Front than the atmosphere of decay that hung over it. No honest writer of memoirs could ignore it: Barbusse described it graphically in *Le Feu*, Arthur Græme West tried to capture it in poetry, and time and again reference is made to it by soldiers in their private correspondence. Battle conditions often made it impossible to bury the dead in a fiercely contested area sometimes for weeks on end and the troops were obliged to live in close proximity to them. Many who were buried suffered an untimely and grisly resurrection through a bursting shell, a land subsidence or a digging party, and many became visibly assimilated into the squelching mud. There was no escaping the sight or smell of this putrescence. Owen defines it elsewhere:

> . . . when bones and the dead are smelt

Under the mud where long ago they fell
Mixed with the sour sharp odour of the shell.

And yet, in that Aceldama, cut off from all the more con-
genial aspects of civilisation and living in what the modern
soldier aptly designates 'foxholes', many felt themselves in
singularly close touch with nature, and nature, despite all
man's savagery, seemed thriving. Indomitably, whenever
the absence of shell-fire permitted it, trees grew, grass came
up and birds sang. On earlier battlefields crops flourished;
in forward areas the size of the rats became well-nigh
phenomenal, and everywhere the poppies of Flanders
nodded their blood-coloured heads. It was impossible to
resist the natural inference. Hamlet might let 'imagination
trace the noble dust of Alexander, till he find it stopping a
bung-hole', but then Hamlet had never shared a mess-tin
with Alexander. Many must have echoed his thought: 'To
what base uses we may return, Horatio!' but for the sake of
sanity this speculation was not to be pushed too far when
'we' included one's friends, the men beside whom one
fought, marched, and did fatigues, and when the least repulsive of the 'base uses' was acting in this fertilising capacity.
In short, faced with this contrast between decaying man and
flourishing nature, what more natural solution for a sensitive
man than the euphemising of this process into a belief that
man after death does become part of the universal spirit and
does, spiritually as well as physically, become 'one with
nature, herb and stone'? At least it provided a grain of
consolation and that was too precious to waste. A psycholo-
gist might contend that it 'satisfies the counter movement of
feeling towards the surrender of personal claims and the
merging of the ego within a greater power —the "community consciousness"', which is what Miss Maud Bodkin
sees as one of the functions of the tragic hero's death, but

whether one uses those or simpler terms one is bound to recognise a unificatory and regenerative value dominating the guilt-association of Owen's blood-imagery.

That Owen derived this in part from his religious up-bringing, as well as from his reading of Romantic poetry, is clearly established in 'Strange Meeting':

> I would have poured my spirit without stint
> But not through wounds; not on the cess of war.
> Foreheads of men have bled where no wounds were.

The implied reference to Christ's 'agony and bloody sweat' is inescapable, illuminating, and wholly successful, but I wish to defer consideration of the Christian element in Owen's work and to turn first to one final value that he gives to this sacrificial aspect of the blood-image. In 'Apologia pro Poemate Meo' it becomes a symbol of the fellowship by which the soldier and his comrades are held to-gether, 'bound with the bandage of the arm that drips'. There is a directly parallel passage in Robert Graves's 'Two Fusiliers':

> Show me the two so closely bound
> As we, by the wet bond of blood,
> By friendship blossoming from mud.
> By Death.

The parallelism is increased by the earlier line 'By wire and wood and stake we're bound', (Owen, also in the 'Apolo-gia', has friendship 'wound with war's hard wire whose stakes are strong'), so that one wonders whether Owen, writing the 'Apologia' at Craiglockhart in 1917, had seen Graves's poem (sent perhaps to Sassoon to whom it would appear to be addressed) and whether that accounts for the 'too' in his opening line: 'I, too, saw God through mud'. Owen was forced by circumstances of war to join the

> wise, who with a thought besmirch
> Blood over all our soul

but the wisdom which those lines from 'Insensibility' attribute to the imaginative apprehension of the many values of 'the wet bond of blood' is richly exemplified throughout his poetry.

II

One of the last comments on his own poetry that Owen ever made to Siegfried Sassoon is contained in a letter of 22 September 1918: 'I don't want to write anything to which a soldier would say *No compris!*' By his echoing of the current army slang as much as by the statement itself Owen indicates the solidarity that he had come to feel with the men under his command. On his first arrival in Flanders his immediate reaction was to identify them with the popular cartoons: 'The men are just as Bairnsfather has them—expressionless lumps. We feel the weight of them hanging on us.' This on 4 January 1917; in November of the same year he wrote his 'Apologia', having shared 'With them in hell the sorrowful dark of hell' and come to recognise that 'These men are worth/Your tears'. Though there may be some idealisation of the relationship in that poem, there is no idealisation of the men themselves, who curse, scowl, and murder, and whose 'foulness' is redeemed only temporarily by their 'passion of oblation'.

A small group of Owen's poems might be called poems of dramatic description, and in all of them the men are presented with this same honesty of vision. Such a poem as 'The Chances' makes it clear that if the soldier's reply in 'Inspection' is lacking in verisimilitude this is not because of any inability on Owen's part to handle ordinary speech in poetry. Where in Kipling, for example, one is conscious at times that the poet is affecting a dialect, in Owen the usage is so much more naturally idiomatic as to be taken for granted, especially in its command of army slang. 'The Chances' relies on slang for its atmosphere of knowingness, half-amused resignation, easy banter, and sardonic understatement until in the last four lines a new, more emotive communication is achieved by the tacit abandoning of slang so that the solitary epithet in the last line receives added weight and intensifies the protest:

> But poor young Jim, 'e's livin' an' 'e's not;
> 'E reckoned 'e'd five chances, an' 'e 'ad;
> 'E's wounded, killed, and pris'ner, all the lot,
> The bloody lot all rolled in one. Jim's mad.

That this is intentional is illustrated by the progressive strengthening of the manuscript versions of that line: 'The old, old lot' gives way to 'the 'ole damn lot', then 'the ruddy lot' and finally 'the bloody lot', although until 1931 'ruddy' had always been printed.

An unpublished poem similar to this is 'The Letter' in which a soldier's letter to his wife is interspersed with verbal asides to his companions. The poem culminates in a surprise bombardment in which the letter-writer is mortally wounded and leaves to his friend the completion of the letter. Although there is some confusion between the spoken and written idiom, there is as in 'The Chances' a keen ear for the soldier's general blasphemy of utterance, his tendency to hyperbolical abuse, and the exasperated pettinesses of which he is capable, but these are effectively contrasted with the cheerful mendacity by which he tries to convince his wife of his complete safety; his rough expressions of consolatory tenderness and his solicitude for her financial position are convincingly expressed in the semi-articulate phraseology of the unpractised letter-writer. The total dramatic effect is corroborative of the view of the men embodied in such poems as 'Insensibility' and 'Apologia', a view that is realistic, wide in its scope, sympathetic and essentially human.

III

It is these same qualities, derived from the same sources of experience and first-hand observation, that characterise Owen's attitude to death in these poems, and to that attitude in particular no soldier 'would say *No compris!*'. The brevity with which 'The Chances' disposes of the man who 'got the knock-out, blown to chops' is, in the apparent brutality of its vernacular bluntness, symptomatic: the clean-cut finality of death occasions no anxiety, especially when it is, as in this case, instantaneous, or when, as in 'Asleep',

> in the happy no-time of his sleeping
> Death took him by the heart.

In some circumstances death is even welcome, and thus of the suicide in 'S.I.W.' it can 'truthfully' and unemotionally be recorded that 'Tim died smiling'. Certainly death is preferable to the physical mutilation described in 'Disabled' and 'A Terre', the gas poisoning of 'Dulce et Decorum Est', the blinding of 'The Sentry', and the terrible agony of 'Mental Cases'; these to the soldier are the causes of fear more potent than death. Although to the present-day reader after two world wars this may appear self-evident to the point of obviousness, it was not so widely realised in 1917, nor was it a familiar element in poetry. Robert Graves's war poetry in expressing what he himself called 'a frank fear of physical death' had struck a new note of faithfulness to fact but his

poetry, like much of Blunden's, is particularly memorable
for its capturing of the soldier's perennial ability to derive a
consolatory amusement and protection from the trivial, the
unexpected or the inconsequential occurrence. Fear is held
at bay as long as possible by a sense of humour or a sense of
'friendship, blossoming from mud'. In Sassoon fear is sometimes frankly recognised and vividly presented (as in 'Attack
or 'The Rear-Guard'), sometimes transmuted into satiric
anger. A comparison of 'Does it matter?' with 'Disabled'
will show how Sassoon's indignation at civilian callousness
withdraws the emphasis from the psychological effect of
mutilation that Owen so fearlessly and feelingly explores:

> Now he will never feel again how slim
> Girls' waists are, or how warm their subtle hands;
> All of them touch him like some queer disease.

It is against this background that the buoyancy of 'The Next
War' must be understood. Its confident assertion that
'Death was never enemy of ours' has its basis in actuality
but it must not obscure the recognition in the closing lines
that in another and more important sense death is still the
last enemy. The 'greater war' of which Owen speaks in
those lines—

> when each proud fighter brags
> He wars on Death—for Life; not men—for flags

—is the war with which Owen's finest poetry is vitally concerned, and it is in this war that the pity for suffering
humanity which he had learnt in the war in Flanders was to
become so important a weapon.

In 'Futility', an elegy for one soldier, unnamed and not
individualised, becomes more even than a requiem for the

war-dead. It opens on a subdued note of saddened but not extinguished faith:

> Move him into the sun—
> Gently its touch awoke him once,
> At home, whispering of fields unsown.
> Always it woke him, even in France,
> Until this morning and this snow.

From this, by a natural and easy transition, it moves towards the weary resentment of

> O what made fatuous sunbeams toil
> To break earth's sleep at all?

The wealth of scorn implicit in 'fatuous'—an epithet that Hardy might well have chosen in a similar context—and the bitterness of the whole couplet seem close to the Sophoclean 'Not to have been born at all were best', but that is not the point of this poem. Sophocles, having reached a conclusion, makes a statement where Owen asks—and leaves unanswered—a question. The lines that precede it are a reassertion of the value of life:

> Are limbs, so dear-achieved, are sides,
> Full-nerved—still warm—too hard to stir?

True pity implies a code of values: you can only pity a person when you can visualise better conditions that have been denied him. Sophocles pities the living for not being dead: Owen pities the dead for not being alive. The very means by which he expresses that in 'Futility', the controlled sensuousness of his emphasis on physical life—limbs, sides, sinews, and warmth—are evidence of a positive belief. We are deliberately invited to 'Think, how it wakes the seeds', to think, in other words, of the process of organic development at which he hints in the imagery of 'Wild with all regrets':

Spring air would find its own way to my lung,
And grow me legs as quick as lilac-shoots.

Imagery of spring and natural growth is prominent in
Owen's poetry because spring itself is also engaged in a war
'on Death—for Life', and much of Owen's most memorable
work is in those poems where this natural parallel is most
imaginatively exploited. In the early poem 'The Seed' he
tries to see the war as itself part of this regenerative process:

But now the exigent winter, and the need
Of sowings for new spring, and flesh for seed.

Blunden's comment that this 'was his reading of the War
as an abstract subject' is confirmed by the more mature and
strikingly different use he makes of similar imagery in
'Futility', 'A Terre', and 'Spring Offensive'.

IV

His poems of dramatic description have an historic and
documentary significance in the vividness of their presentation of the actuality of trench warfare and the suffering it
caused; his poems of personal response (such as 'the Calls',
'Apologia' and 'Greater Love') are deeply moving in the
eloquent directness of their sincerity of feeling and honesty
of expression; but his poems of imaginative description are
in many ways more far-reaching in their implications and
more satisfactory as poetry. These poems do not attempt the
direct, generalised philosophical summing up that is represented by the personal poems, but the incident or scene
is here subjected to a more extensive modification by the
poetic imagination than in the poems of dramatic description. They do not seek to present an illusion of actuality by
means of realistic speech: there is no dialogue in them at all.

They do not put forward one clearly defined episode and leave us to decide how far that is representative of war. 'Exposure' is not localised except in its application to trench warfare: it could be a record of the thoughts of any soldiers on the Western Front, on either side of No Man's Land, at almost any period of the war. 'Spring Offensive' suggests no one particular attack but many, and 'The Send-Off,' though it too may be based on experience, is similarly universalised:

> So secretly, like wrongs hushed-up, they went.
> They were not ours:
> We never heard to which front these were sent.

A good example of this process is the composition of 'Asleep'. An unpublished letter to his cousin, with whom he had spent a day's leave on 14 November 1917 near Winchester, describes how, as he walks back to Winchester alone across the downs in the dusk, his imagination unexpectedly visualises the trenches with such vividness that he can 'almost see the dead lying about in the hollows of the downs'. This poem is an imaginative concentration on one of these figures, a man killed in his sleep, and is clearly a recollection in tranquillity of the emotion Owen must have experienced on some occasion in France, but what matters is not the mere interval in time between the experience and the poem. Some of the poems of dramatic description are just as distanced in time and space from the events they describe— 'The Sentry', on which he was working in September 1918 is clearly based on an incident outlined in a letter of 16 January 1917—but these poems seek to maintain an illusion of contemporaneity with the event to which such poems as 'Asleep' do not pretend. The vision on the downs indicates how the poetic imagination has, by the Coleridgean process

74

of dissolving, diffusing, and dissipating, re-created the original experience. The externals are briefly indicated in the first nine lines; no localising background is given, no attempt made to individualise the sleeper: like the dead soldier in 'Futility' he is the prototype of the Unknown Warrior:

> Under his helmet, up against his pack,
> After the many days of work and waking,
> Sleep took him by the brow and laid him back.

In the imaginative process of re-creation the individual and the episode become universalised. Consideration of the dead soldier gives way to speculation about death, but such speculation is constantly and carefully related to its source. Not only does the grammatical structure of the poem's second paragraph ensure a return to the dead soldier, but the grandiloquent vision of heaven,

> the shaking
> Of great wings, and the thoughts that hung the stars,
> High pillowed on calm pillows of God's making
> Above these clouds, these rains,

is immediately checked by the ambivalent image 'these sheets of lead' (a leaden-coloured sleety day, or the 'hail' of lead bullets) which prepares us for the unmistakably war-like image of the wind's scimitars. (Compare, in 'Exposure', 'the merciless east winds that knive us'). So too in the next four lines Owen contrives at once to underpin metaphysical speculation with inescapable physical fact:

> —Or whether yet his thin and sodden head
> Confuses more and more with the low mould,
> His hair being one with the grey grass
> And finished fields of autumns that are old. . . .

In the insistence here on bleak desolation, dampness, and decomposition (intensified by the verb 'confuses') Owen is rejecting the consolation of the 'Tommy's creed' of 'pushing up daisies' in order to emphasise his main theme of death. The feigned indifference with which speculation is broken off—'Who knows? Who hopes? Who troubles? Let it pass'—indicates by its telling sequence of verbs the emotional gradations and the ironic, preparing us for the ambivalence of the last two lines which have the appearance of purely factual statement: 'He sleeps'; but which by their reiteration and expansion of the statement bring us back to life:

> He sleeps less tremulous, less cold,
> Than we who must awake, and waking, say Alas!

What is so sadly wrong is not that we must awake but that we must awake to such grief. The poem, far from being morbidly obsessed with the dead, is ultimately much more disturbed about the living: the state of the dead needs less pity than that of the living but the terms in which it is presented effectively preclude our feeling that death is in any absolute sense desirable, however tempting it may appear for the moment. Though death may be seen as befriending this particular soldier, Owen leaves us in no doubt that death is the poet's enemy on whom the poet has to war— 'for Life'.

A less successful instance of a similar creative process at work is to be found in the sonnet 'Hospital Barge at Cérisy'. The octave presents us with the objectified description of the scene, the sestet relates the scene to the onlooker and tries to universalise it imaginatively by linking it with the passing of Arthur, but the two parts are inadequately integrated, and it is Fancy rather than Imagination that is at work. In the first part the barge is portrayed with rather too much detail (a mistake he does not make in 'Asleep'):

> Softly her engines down the current screwed
> And chuckled in her . . .
> The lock-gate took her bulging amplitude.
> Gently into the gurgling lock she swum.

The one phrase intended presumably to act as a precursor of the changed note of the sestet, 'fairy tinklings', is too much at variance with the realistic note of the rest of the description. This realism also makes the inaccuracy of 'her *funnel* screamed' more discordant, and the final transition to Arthur, euphonious as it is, a little self-conscious. Its literariness seems artificial and overwrought by comparison with the spontaneity and intensity of first-hand emotion that informs most of his work, but its method is, with this exception, the same as in the other poems of imaginative description.

V

There are two fundamental antitheses common to most of these poems, the contrast between two states of being (the present and the past, as in 'Exposure' and 'Hospital Barge'; the present and the problematical future, as in the artillery sonnet and 'The Send-Off'), and the contrast between life and death (as in 'Asleep, 'Futility', and 'Spring Offensive'). Coupled with this and related to it is a greater preoccupation with eternity than Owen has displayed in either of the other two groups. Here he is enlarging his work to enable it to cope with the great poetic verities that he had tentatively sought after in his juvenilia. What attracts him in these poems is death, not simply as death, not merely as an end of life, but as a state of transition between two existences.

It is this that the poem which Blunden entitles 'Fragment:

A Farewell' records, and again it is pregnant with much more meaning than might at first appear. This description of death is at first sight more ornate than Owen usually allows himself to be, but it is a much more disciplined poem than any of his juvenilia. The sensuousness of the opening is relaxed in a way unusual in Owen when writing of blood:

> I saw his round mouth's crimson deepen as it fell,
> Like a Sun, in his last deep hour.

This, the only hint of war, in the poem, contrasts so markedly with his description of wounds elsewhere that we are instantly prepared for something different. The imagery, too, which in so many of his poems is belittling and calculated to shock, is here expansive, Romantic. Elsewhere nature is compared to man and the works of man, as in the lines of 'Exposure':

> Dawn, massing in the East her melancholy army,
> Attacks once more in ranks on shivering ranks of gray

with their magnificent dual suggestion of dawn breaking and of a German dawn attack; and nature and death are linked only in ugliness, as they are in this fragment:

> Cramped in that funnelled hole, they watched the dawn
> Open a jagged rim around; a yawn
> Of death's jaws, which had all but swallowed them
> Stuck in the middle of his throat of phlegm.

In 'A Farewell', however, the process is reversed; it achieves its unity by its consistently cosmic imagery. The dying man is pictured in terms of the universe: 'like a Sun', 'clouding', 'the heavens of his cheek', 'cold stars' and 'skies'; and yet paradoxically this magnification of the individual does not produce any sense of exaltation. The first five lines maintain an equilibrium—they are indeed 'half gleam, half glower'—

but in the last three the image, being more fully developed, takes charge and the occasion of the image, the eyes, is dwarfed by the stern grandeur of the last two lines:

> The cold stars lighting, very old and bleak
> In different skies.

The emotion has been transferred from the subject to the image: it is not a man that is dying, but a universe, and language that might have been used to make this microcosm's death sublime has instead been employed to conjure up a chilling vision of a doomed world. There is added force in the suggestion that the last line carries of 'indifferent skies': the play on words may be as grimly deliberate as the near-pun on curse and corpses at the beginning of 'The Sentry'. This is no more hopeful, no more Christian, a poem than 'The End' which it recalls, but its compactness and technique, its masterly control of language and movement, make it much superior to 'The End'. In its brevity there is a self-contained unity and an evocative power to which Blunden's title 'Fragment' does less than justice. The very doubt that it is intended to communicate preordains a sense of incompleteness, but its organic coherence, as well as its manuscript (an untitled fair copy with only one small amendment), contradict the idea of fragmentariness.

The best of these poems that seem on the brink of two worlds is 'Spring Offensive'. It sustains the distinction made in 'Insensibility' between those who, having lost imagination, can sleep carelessly in the shade of 'a last hill', and the others more sensitive who

> stood still
> To face the stark, blank sky beyond the ridge,
> Knowing their feet had come to the end of the world.

The stark blankness of this sky may strengthen the interpretation of indifferent skies in the final line of the poem just discussed, for like that poem, 'Spring Offensive' rests on a number of antitheses of which this is one. Another is the contrast between the unnaturalness of what these men are doing and the natural background against which they are doing it. Contrasted with some of the attempts by other poets considered in Chapter One at a similar evocation of natural beauty, these lines provide an excellent example of how, by deliberately stripping it of personal associations and allusions, Owen avoids sentimentalising the theme. This can and does pass as a reflection of the mood of soldiers before an attack, but it is also a clear instance of how the poetic imagination has transmuted the experience of others, giving it at once universality and yet the quality of an intensely personal vision. The inversion 'Marvelling they stood' throws into immediate prominence the keynote of beauty-inspired wonder. The generalised picture of

> the long grass swirled
> By the May breeze, murmurous with wasp and midge

is evocative but not limiting—each reader can relate it to a scene he knows and his confidence is increased by the almost Pre-Raphaelite selection of significant detail. Only then does Owen's imagination take charge, unobtrusively, but for the alert reader unmistakably:

> For though the summer oozed into their veins
> Like an injected drug for their bodies' pains . . .

The modern, clinical image, arresting and yet perfectly appropriate, gives individuality to a belief in 'the healing power of Nature' and helps to remove any objection to it as an automatic literary convention. Here again is the blood symbol and Owen's sense of the oneness of all created life, the indestructible unity between man and nature: 'Summer *oozed into their veins*' (and the simile that follows heightens the literalness of this), 'Sharp *on their souls* hung the imminent line of grass', 'the *warm* field', the brambles 'clutched and clung to them *like sorrowing hands*', 'They breathe *like trees* unstirred'.

In this poem, with its packed wealth of suggestion, Owen's technique is at its most mature. The tense, apprehensive mood of the soldiers is well indicated by their geographical position, the 'blank sky beyond the ridge' contrasted with the certainty of 'the far valley behind', and the powerful suggestion of 'the imminent line of grass', while their reluctance to leave this comfortable, known, natural world is hinted at merely in 'their *slow* boots coming up'. The tempo, too, is skilfully varied from the meditative slowness of the opening three stanzas, working up through the tension of the fourth to the exhilarating action of

> So, soon they topped the hill, and raced together
> Over an open stretch of herb and heather
> Exposed.

The heavy caesura after 'Exposed' heralds the dramatic abruptness with which the counter-fire bursts on attackers and readers alike:

> And instantly the whole sky burned
> With fury against them; earth set sudden cups
> In thousands for their blood; and the green slope
> Chasmed and steepened sheer to infinite space.

A row of dots then preludes the return to the meditative note for the conclusion. Admirable too is the way in which the actual attack is presented in terms of the scene already described. The blankness of the sky gives way to positive hatred—'the whole sky burned/With fury against them'—but earth is still friendly, and the buttercups, their blessing unavailing, are recalled in grimmer context in the allusion to the shell-holes: 'earth set sudden cups/In thousands for their blood'; and the hill ridge has become the brink of consciousness:

> and the green slope
> Chasmed and steepened sheer to infinite space.

More perhaps than any of his other poems, 'Spring Offensive' in its alternation between life and death does convey imaginatively the nervous tension of the soldier in moments of crisis. Other poets have described an attack, seeing it as exhilarating or terrifying according to their temperaments; it is characteristic of Owen that he should concern himself also with the lasting effects of such an attack on the survivors. The spring to which they come 'crawling slowly back' still arouses wonder in them, but it is not the same spring nor the same wonder as those of the earlier stanzas. They have their own secret, their reluctance, even inability, to speak of 'comrades that went under', and if Owen offers no reason for this it is because he has already answered his own question in the sonnet 'Happiness'. The survivors, having besmirched 'blood over all their souls', can no longer see their world as it was: the buttercups have become receptacles for blood, not givers of benisons:

> The sun may cleanse
> And time, and starlight . . .
> But the old Happiness is unreturning.

In an unpublished letter of 27 November 1917 he drew Sassoon's attention to an image in a poem by his cousin and identified it as his own; it is a felicitous reference to young bracken:

> Like carven croziers are the curled shoots growing
> To bless me as I pass.

The recurrence of this idea in the buttercup image in 'Spring Offensive' is paralleled by another echo: in 'The Unreturning' 'the indefinite, unshapen dawn' had led the poet to a dread of 'a heaven with doors so chained', and in 'Spring Offensive' 'the stark, blank sky' is markedly contrasted with the rich organic unity of man and nature. The hostile menace of the dawn in 'Exposure' and 'Mental Cases' is directly related to conditions of war, but the line, 'Fearfully flashed the sky's mysterious glass', is closer to the dawn of 'The Unreturning' in its suggestion of a supernatural hostility symbolised by the sky itself. The antithesis between the unsympathetic impenetrability of the sky and the luminous warmth of the sun is inescapable in the reference to the waiting soldiers:

> . . . eyes that faced
> The sun, like a friend with whom their love is done.
> O larger shone that smile against the sun,
> Mightier than his whose bounty these have spurned.

As in 'Futility' the sun is a life force, a creative principle from which the soldier is cut off, but this time it is by an act of deliberate rejection. The insistence, in the final stanzas of 'Spring Offensive', on imagery of hell and damnation, as well as the calculated doubt and hesitancy of '*Some say* God caught them', introduces an ethical note not present in 'Futility'. The sense of alienation in 'Spring Offensive' is the more terrible because it is the result of active choice, not passive suffering, and because it reflects so keenly the schism in Owen's own soul.

CHAPTER FIVE

The Very Seared Conscience

IN all Owen's writing no phrase is more revelatory than
his description of himself as 'a conscientious objector with
a very seared conscience', which occurs in the important
letter where he records poignantly his realisation that 'pure
Christianity will not fit in with pure patriotism'. Already in
his earliest poetry we have seen an uneasiness over religious
belief finding expression in a somewhat derivative idiom
that detracts from its spontaneity, but of the intensity of the
spiritual crisis into which his participation in the war
plunged him there can be no doubt. The sense of guilt and
of divided responsibility that I have indicated in 'Mental
Cases', 'Spring Offensive', and elsewhere is best formulated
by Owen himself in a letter to Osbert Sitwell of 4 July 1918
from Scarborough that parallels 'Inspection':

> For fourteen hours yesterday I was at work—teaching Christ
> to lift his cross by numbers, and how to adjust his crown;
> and not to imagine he thirst till after the last halt; I attended
> his Supper to see that there were no complaints; and inspected
> his feet that they should be worthy of the nails. I see to it that
> he is dumb and stands at attention before his accusers. With a
> piece of silver I buy him every day, and with maps I make
> him familiar with the topography of Golgotha.

The significance of that elaborate metaphor lies in the role
the writer assigns to himself: he is in every instance betray-
ing the Christ-soldier and thus alienating himself from the
mercy of Christ.

Such popularly-accepted phrases as 'the supreme sacrifice'

illustrate how readily the soldier came to be thought of in a role similar to that of the crucified Saviour. One of the few successful poetic versions of this identification is Sassoon's 'The Redeemer', but too many poems of what I have called 'the personal phase' of Great War poetry suffer by the over-frequency of analogies with the Crucifixion. The 1914 certainty that God was on our side survives in the work of many of these young men in the form of an emotional religiosity and a sense of personal kinship with Christ; this may have been of value to them as individuals but not as poets, since it has the effect of shutting their eyes to the real significance of what is happening around them without correspondingly increasing their powers as meditative or religious poets. The basis of this identification is, of course, the scriptural text which Owen quotes in the following form in the letter speaking of his seared conscience, and again at the end of 'At a Calvary' (it also gave him the title for one of his most deeply-felt poems): 'Greater love hath no man than this, that a man lay down his life for a friend'; but the same letter contains the realisation that the soldier who makes this sacrifice may in the course of so doing disobey 'one of Christ's essential commands ... do not kill'. This paradoxical concept has been memorably defined by Alex Comfort: 'The Promethean Infantryman, both Christ and Crucifier'; and the greatness of 'Strange Meeting' lies, in part, in the success with which it (like 'The Show') develops the *doppelgänger* theme as a perfect symbol of this dichotomy. Since this religious problem underlies so much of Owen's poetry it is not extravagant to see a possible reference to Christ in the sun 'whose bounty these have spurned' in 'Spring Offensive', for ignoring the 'essential commandment' is tantamount to spurning the salvation Christianity offers.

85

This is not to attribute to Owen in these poems a wholly orthodox Christian view. In 'At a Calvary near the Ancre' he is as much at odds with the 'pulpit professionals' as in the letter on pacifism, but in both cases his accusation is that Christ has been betrayed by His Church. In 'Le Christianisme', a more balanced, ironic poem, the inadequacy and remoteness of the Church is neatly epitomised in the lines

> In cellars, packed-up saints lie serried
> Well out of hearing of our trouble.

In this sentiment Owen was by no means alone. The religious assurance of earlier war poets was dying out by 1917: Christ in Flanders was too much of a paradox to be easily accepted any longer. Some, like Arthur Græme West, professed atheism; others retained a nominal adherence to Christianity but found its consolation failing. C. E. Montague's chapter 'The sheep that were not fed' in *Disenchantment* is very relevant here, particularly his quotation of the New Army recruit's comment 'I've been a Christian all my life, but this war is a bit too serious'. Typical is the end of Sassoon's 'To any Dead Officer': 'Good-bye, old lad! Remember me to God' where the irreverent casualness masks a more serious innuendo. Many of the men in France were becoming increasingly convinced that they needed 'remembering' to a God who had forgotten them. Warmongering bishops (as in 'They'), who told them 'The ways of God are strange' had ceased to command their belief or their respect; whatever they may have said on Church Parade, Sassoon echoed the real—if unspoken—prayers of many in 'Stand-to: Good Friday Morning':

> O Jesus, send me a wound today,
> And I'll believe in Your bread and wine,
> And get my bloody old sins washed white!

Analogies with the Crucifixion now acquired a more bitter note as in Osbert Sitwell's epigram, much admired by Owen, which ends:

> They gave Him vinegar, and pierced His side,
> But Clemenceau was fully satisfied!

Yet it would be unjust to dismiss these men as irreverent, godless, and blasphemous. Their agnosticism is the product of their circumstances and often conceals, as in West's case, a very real desire to believe. The frequent invocation of Christ ('O Jesu, make it stop!' or the final lines of 'The Redeemer', for example, from Sassoon) suggests something deeper than army blasphemy, and the tendency to draw on Biblical stories for satires is surely an indication of how prominent their old faith was in their minds, even if they found temporary difficulty in reconciling it with their circumstances. Thus the sacrifice of Isaac by Abraham provided both Osbert Sitwell and Owen with a theme, while Sassoon draws on the story of Cain and Abel. That these are Old Testament stories is not unconnected with the fact that whereas the 'bardic' poets had usually invoked God in their patriotic poetry, it is to Christ that the later poets more frequently appeal.

The significance of this is nowhere better illustrated than in Owen's unpublished 'Soldier's Dream', a pungent eight-line poem of 1917 in which a soldier dreams of the war ending by the personal intervention of 'kind Jesus' in putting all weapons out of action. The peace, however, is short-lived:

> But God was vexed, and gave all power to Michael;
> And when I woke he'd seen to our repairs.

God, that is, has been identified with Jahveh, the Old

Testament God of battles and of wrath, whose interest in the perpetuation of the war is sharply contrasted with the compassion of Christ who, as Divinity incarnate, can sympathise with the human suffering war involves. In the face of this prolongation of suffering neither victory nor death has any great significance. The war that Jahveh wishes for is death, the death of the spirit, whereas the compassion represented by Christ is life-giving and kind, like the sun in 'Futility' and in 'Spring Offensive' where the antithesis between the sun, 'the friend with whom their love is done', and the 'stark, blank sky' full of incipient menace and hostility may be a reflection of this antithesis between Christ and God.

Questionable as its theology may be, Owen's position here is one to which many must, in varying degrees, have been attracted (it finds expression also, for example, in Jules Romains's novel *Verdun*), and it is one for which the Church was itself partly to blame because of the ardent and uncritical support it appeared to give to the continuance of the war. As late as November 1921 *The Nation* reviewed the memoirs of an army chaplain (entitled *Happy Days in France and Flanders*) with considerable acerbity for the 'absence of protest and indignation' and for its unquestioning acceptance of such incidents of war as the execution for desertion of a twenty-year-old soldier with four years' service. It is hardly surprising that Owen's poetry should contain such statements as 'God seems not to care' and 'love of God seems dying', though his refusal to word either of them more dogmatically indicates the strength of the religion in which he had been brought up.

II

Owen's pacifism, however, although usually expressed in Christian terms, is not entirely the outcome of the conflict between his military experience and his religious upbringing. There is another influence behind it, more powerful than is sometimes recognised. During his stay in Bordeaux he had made the acquaintance of the French poet Laurent Tailhade who was at that time fifty-nine. That, despite the discrepancy between their ages, a real friendship seems to have developed between them is pleasantly illustrated by a photograph of them holding a book between them and with the older man's arm round Owen's shoulder, as well as by the whole tone of a letter from Tailhade to Owen published in Paris in 1939 which ends 'Wilfred, je vous embrasse bien affectueusement, votre vieil ami, Laurent Tailhade'; 'affectueusement' is substituted for the more formal 'amicalement' originally written and then crossed out. The letter refers to Owen's comments on Tailhade's volume of verse *Les Fleurs d'Ophélie* and suggests that Owen should translate them into English verse, but it is not as a poet that Tailhade most significantly influenced his young English friend. Originally intended for the Church, Tailhade had early in life revolted against Christianity but was none the less a confirmed pacifist who had been in considerable trouble with the authorities for his *Lettre aux Conscrits* (1903). This and his address *Pour la Paix*, delivered in 1908 and reprinted with the other piece in 1909, anticipate Owen so markedly in sentiment and even on occasion in turns of expression that it is impossible that Owen should not have known them. The definition of poetry in *Pour la Paix* is very close indeed to the conception of it that underlies Owen's draft preface:

La poésie elle-même n'est autre chose qu'une invocation magnanime, un *sursum corda* vers la fraternité.

In the same work his description of soldiers as 'les tragiques moissonneurs de cadavres' and his frequent use of 'hécatombes' (which Owen was to employ inaccurately in 'The Kind Ghosts') find echoes in the work of the English poet; while such a passage as the following reference to civilisation after the fall of the Roman Empire is full of associations:

La nuit se fait bientôt. Une aurore de ténèbres obscurcit l'horizon. C'est le brouillard, le froid, l'hiver, une obscurité sanglante peuplée de monstres et de fantômes. Des larves rampent sur le sol. Accroupie au bord du chemin, la Sottise rabâche et déraisonne. Çà et là, des ombres équivoques s'entredéchirent dans le chaos.

If the imagery of the last two sentences suggests 'Mental Cases', the sentence 'Des larves rampent sur le sol' is curiously close to 'The Show', with its somewhat uncommon use of the verb 'ramped'

> Across its beard, that horror of harsh wire,
> There moved thin caterpillars, slowly uncoiled
>
> .   .   .   .   .
>
> Those that were gray, of more abundant spawn,
> Ramped on the rest and ate them and were eaten.

In the *Lettre aux Conscrits* the older generation is blamed for the sacrifice of the younger and Owen's awareness of a brotherhood transcending the barriers of nationalism is anticipated in such a passage as this:

Ces ennemis, coupables seulement d'être nés sur le versant d'une colline, sur la berge d'une fleuve qui sépare leurs champs du tien, ces ennemis, dont le tort le plus clair est de se nommer Frantz quand tu t'appelles François, ils ont les mêmes intérêts,

les mêmes affections qui te pressent. Ils ont, là-bas, des com-
pagnes, leur mère et des amis dont les yeux se mouillèrent au
départ. Ils aiment, eux aussi, la clarté du soleil et le parfum des
bois. Ils portent dans leurs veines le sang pourpré de la jeun-
esse. Ils s'avancent, comme toi, pleins de vie, à la conquête du
bonheur.

Without too reckless an attribution of 'influences' one can
say with safety that Tailhade's pacifist beliefs must have
made on Owen an impression so deep that particular phrases
and images may well have remained at some level of his
consciousness, but more important is the fact that Tailhade
must have introduced Owen to such ideas as those epito-
mized in the following passage:

Or tes parents sont lâches. Ils défèrent au mensonge de la
Patrie et permettent sans horreur que tu t'en ailles 'sous les
drapeaux'. Si bien que tu n'es pas à présent la chair à travail
de l'usine, mais la chair à tuerie de la caserne, l'organe imper-
sonnel dans la mécanique détestable qui, sous le nom d'armée
et sous prétexte de défense publique, annihile tout ce que les
hommes de ton âge portent dans le coeur et l'esprit de bon,
de généreux et de sensé.

Reste maître de toi-même. Ne consens jamais à des actes que,
libre et seul juge de tes actions, tu regarderais comme infâmes
et scélérats.

Ne tue pas! Et, si l'on te prescrit de tuer refuse d'obéir cette
fois, comme les Quakers d'Angleterre et les Doukhobors de
Russie! Ne tue pas! C'est la loi, non chrétienne, mais universelle, précepte d'amour et de solidarité que nul ne peut abroger,
mais que tous doivent accomplir.

What Tailhade is preaching here is not mutiny or sedition
so much as liberty of conscience: much the same thing

might be said of Owen's later differentiation between God
and Christ. Tailhade's pacifist influence, however, was not
strong enough in 1915, when the call for volunteers was
becoming more clamorous and urgent, to deter Owen from
returning home to enlist; it was characteristic of Tailhade's
wise tolerance that his letter on the eve of Owen's departure
should have contained no word of reproach, no reiteration
of pacifist principles: his young friend had made his own
choice and was following his own conscience. When, two
years later, that conscience had become 'very seared' it
must have been of inestimable value to Owen to recall Tailhade's lesson that morality was not the exclusive prerogative
of any one church and not indissolubly wedded to formal
religion, but that some laws might well be universal.

III

This, after all, is the theme of 'The Calls':

> I heard the sighs of men, that have no skill
> To speak of their distress, no, nor the will
> A voice I know. And this time I must go.

The only call to which Owen answers is not that of the
church but of human suffering. It is human sympathy rather
than abstract morality that determines his ethical position,
and he reaches that position by a decision as independent, as
courageous, and in some ways as theologically debatable as
that of a fictitious character with whom Owen would at
first sight seem to have little in common. In a situation where
the social and religious codes of his day appear to be at
variance with his own instinctive loyalty to his friend,
Huckleberry Finn puts the humanitarian consideration before the abstract by a choice, the momentousness of which
he expresses to himself in the words 'All right, then, I'll *go*

to hell!' Confronted by a moral problem considerably more complex in its implications but not necessarily any more intensely-realised for that reason, Owen came in effect to a very similar decision, as his letters show time and again. From very different circumstances he learned, like Huck, that 'Human beings *can* be awful cruel to one another'; in the face of this cruelty both of them, obeying the consciences which they affected to regard as compromised, based their conduct on what might well have been described in Tailhade's words: 'la loi, non chrétienne, mais universelle, précepte d'amour et de solidarité que nul ne peut abroger'. In neither case, however, is there anything sentimental about this precept of love and solidarity; *Huckleberry Finn* ends with its hero's despairing withdrawal from a civilisation whose true nature he has come painfully to recognise, just as in 'Strange Meeting' the dead soldier has the courage and the wisdom necessary 'To miss the march of this retreating world'.

The lonely independence of which Huck is the fictional symbol becomes increasingly dominant in Owen's poetry in direct proportion to the increase in his dedication to the task of speaking for 'these boys . . . as well as a pleader can'. His sense of comradeship and solidarity leads to no sentimentally Whitmanesque merging of identity with them, but at the same time his awareness of isolation is more firmly grounded and poetically more valuable than the uneasy Romantic pose of the juvenilia to which it is directly related. The ten-stanza poem, of which 'This is the Track' originally formed the three last (and only revised) verses, develops an image used in a letter to Sassoon in November 1917 ('I was always a mad comet; but you have fixed me'); in the poem he aspires to be a solitary meteor awakening in men premonitions and intimations of eternity. The published stanzas illustrate a similarly purposeful self-sufficiency coupled with an almost messianic belief in the poet's responsibility, the exercise of which may even 'turn aside the very sun', but another and rather better poem of probably similar date puts the other side.

'Six o'clock in Princes St' is just as Tennysonian in origin as is the contemporaneous 'Hospital Barge' sonnet which he described as 'due to a Saturday night revel in "The Passing of Arthur"', but it is more critical of that revel than is 'Hospital Barge'. A half-envious watching of the home-going crowds creates dissatisfaction with his own loneliness and the reflection:

> Neither should I go fooling over clouds,
>   Following gleams unsafe, untrue,
> And tiring after beauty with star-crowds,
>   Dared I go side by side with you.

A letter to Sassoon of 27 November 1917 had parodied Tennyson's 'Merlin and the Gleam':

> I am Owen and I am dying,
> I am Wilfred; and I follow the Gleam

so that the 'gleams unsafe, untrue' may be associated not only with the failing vision of beauty but also with the weakening of religious belief. Certainly the mood is antithetical to that of 'The Fates', written less than six months earlier, with its Georgian confidence in beauty and art as an escape from 'the march of lifetime'; and the choice of the verb 'dared' in the last line shows an honesty of self-knowledge anticipatory of those letters of the following summer in which he told at least two of his friends how glad he was to have been recommended for the Military Cross 'for the confidence it will give me in dealing with civilians'.

The real quality of this poem is most apparent in the final stanza where the poet's isolation is embodied in the wish that he might

> . . . be you on the gutter where you stand,
> Pale rain-flawed phantom of the place,
> With news of all the nations in your hand,
> And all their sorrows in your face.

The newsboy is more than a feature of the Princes Street scene: he is symbolic of the human condition as well as of the war-torn world and, in the pity of the final line, a projection of Owen himself. The effectiveness of the unusual 'rain-flawed' is a reminder of Owen's fondness for and success with elemental imagery and of the progress he has made since the juvenilia in compressing into one line a wealth of association and suggestion.

If this is a poem of which he might have said, as he did of 'Miners', 'but I get mixed up with the War at the end', it resembles 'Miners' also in its development of a symbolist technique as a means of communicating a sense of isolation. There is a richness and complexity about 'Miners' that is quite absent from, for example, so slight a piece as 'The Promisers' and even from ' Winter Song'. The burning coal becomes a symbol for, in turn, the remote past, the miners who dug it, and, by a well-managed and apparently easy but none the less effective transition, the war dead. The atmosphere of the opening stanzas with their leaves, frond-forests, ferns, and birds is reminiscent of 'From My Diary' and the 'Sonnet: to a Child', but where 'From My Diary' contents itself with the creation of that atmosphere and the sonnet associates it pleasantly but conventionally with the ideas of anamnesis and growing old, 'Miners' contrasts it with the 'sourness' of the sacrificed lives (to use Owen's own word for the poem's quality). Out of the oxymoron of this fusion comes a new strength, while the end of the poem gains in emotive force by the unexpected identification of the poet with the suffering of the lost which he has hitherto described detachedly. (It is of course the same device that he uses so effectively in 'The Show', 'Mental Cases', and 'Strange Meeting'.)

> Comforted years will sit soft-chaired
>   In rooms of amber;
> The years will stretch their hands, well-cheered
>   By our lives' ember.
>
> The centuries will burn rich loads
>   With which we groaned,
> Whose warmth shall lull their dreaming lids
>   While songs are crooned.
> But they will not dream of us poor lads
>   Lost in the ground.

The skill with which these two stanzas build up an impression of relaxed luxury, physical ease, and opulent, unquestioning well-being, is epitomised in the phrase 'rooms of amber', where the one word 'amber', apart from its richness of sound, carries immediate associations of wealth and of the warm, golden light suffusing a fire-lit room. But amber, being fossilised resin, is doubly relevant here, for it is produced by the same process as the coal which makes possible all the luxury; this may suggest a secondary association with the insects frequently found imprisoned in amber—cut off, in fact, from the outside world by the amber as effectively as the 'comforted', 'soft-chaired' occupants of these rooms are isolated from reality by the opulence that 'amber' symbolises in this stanza. Thus not only is amber the perfectly appropriate symbol here, but it grows organically out of the rest of the poem. The 'frond-forests' become fossilised into two products: the utilitarian coal, the luxurious, hard amber; so the post-war stability and also the hard-hearted luxury that will again be possible in those more stable conditions are both produced by the war-dead 'lost in the ground'. An exactly parallel idea is sketched in the fragment 'The Abyss of War' but there the pearl imagery is less integrally related to the bronze. 'Miners' moves from the remote past of the forests, emerging from underground into the present, and passing on (by the unobtrusive gradation 'the years . . .' 'the centuries') to the remote future as it returns underground. In other words it has a unifying shape indispensable to the conveying of the total effect, and it uses imagery not decoratively but integrally and functionally with a flexibility and evocative subtlety in the manner of the Symbolists.

Edmund Blunden's observation that Owen 'is, at moments, an English Verlaine', becomes most meaningful in relation to such a poem as 'The Roads Also':

> The old houses muse of the old days
> And their fond trees leaning on them doze,
>
> .   .   .   .   .
>
> Though their own child cry for them in tears,
> Women weep but hear no sound upstairs.
> They believe in loves they had not lived
> And in passion past the reach of the stairs
>   To the world's towers or stars.

This is reminiscent in mood and manner of 'Chanson d'Automne':

> Je me souviens
> Des jours anciens
> Et je pleure

and even more of Verlaine's lyric from *Sagesse* 'Le ciel est, par-dessus le toit'. (In 'The Unreturning' there is a verbal echo from 'Mon Rêve Familier' of the reference to the dead as 'ceux des aimés que la Vie exila'.)

> Rien de plus cher que la chanson grise
> Où l'Indécis au Précis se joint

from Verlaine's 'Art Poétique' is a good description of 'The Roads Also' where the clear definition of images in the earlier part of the poem melts into the frustrated, uneasy melancholy of the last nine lines with their symbolist evocation of a loneliness so complete that even communication is no longer possible. Much of the mood of this poem depends upon its lyrical dream-like movement which again recalls Verlaine:

> De la musique avant toute chose,
> Et pour cela préfère l'Impair

a comment that might almost refer directly to the half-rhyme that is so successfully used here.

Though not specifically war-poems, these, like 'The Kind Ghosts', illustrate Owen's range and may offer some indication of how his poetry might have developed had he lived, but they are important also as examples of the positive though indirect influence on his poetry of the compassion and the sense of isolation induced by his 'very seared conscience'.

IV

In the last chapter I differentiated between two types of poem with which Owen experiments: his poems of dramatic description (such as 'The Chances') and the more subjective lyrics of personal response (such as 'Greater Love' or

'Apologia'). Both have their advantages and their limitations, but what Owen needed for the full attaining of his
purpose was a poetry where the more objective detachment
of the one could be harnessed with the emotional intensity
of the other. He often achieved this in his poems of imaginative description such as 'Spring Offensive' but he also
accomplished it in what I would call poems of visionary
description; of these 'The Show' is a good example, but
'Strange Meeting', the poem that Sassoon once called
Owen's 'passport to immortality, and his elegy to the unknown warriors of all nations', is the best, especially for the
way in which it brings together so many strands of his work
already discussed. Essentially a poem of trench warfare,
realistically based on the First World War, it is a fine statement of Owen's moral idealism as well, but it is also a poem
that shows his true relationship to the Romantic tradition
as something much more positive and creative than his
earlier aestheticism suggests.

This may most readily be seen if a passage in Shelley's
Revolt of Islam (Canto V stanzas ix to xiii inclusive) be
examined with Owen in mind. Wounded in battle, the protagonist hails the flow of blood with rapture because of its
'eloquence which shall not be withstood' and its demon-
stration to his comrades of 'the truth of love's benignant
laws'. He seizes the opportunity to reveal to his fellow-
soldiers the awful significance of what they have blindly
done:

> And those whom love did set his watch to keep
> Around your tents, truth's freedom to bestow,
> Ye stabbed as they did sleep—but they forgive ye now.
>
> Oh wherefore should ill ever flow from ill
> And pain still keener pain for ever breed

> We all are brethren—even the slaves who kill
> For hire, are men.

The closeness of this to 'Strange Meeting' and other poems of Owen's is apparent enough; but it becomes unmistakable when the speaker, having swooned from loss of blood, awakens to find himself 'mid friends and foes':

> And one whose spear had pierced me, leaned beside,
>   With quivering lips and humid eyes;—and all
> Seemed like some brothers on a journey wide
>   Gone forth, whom now strange meeting did befall
>   In a strange land, round one whom they might call
> Their friend, their chief, their father, for assay
>   Of peril, which had saved them from the thrall
> Of death, now suffering. Thus the vast array
> Of those fraternal bands were reconciled that day.

The reconciliation of enemies, the sense of the brotherhood of man, and of the ultimate conquest even of death, as well as the title phrase 'Strange Meeting' are common to both poems, though Owen's is the more closely-knit and the more intensely visualised.

Another parallel may be found towards the end of Keats's *Endymion:*

>   or when in mine
> Far under-ground, a sleeper meets his friends
> Who know him not. Each diligently bends
> Towards common thoughts and things for very fear;
> Striving their ghastly malady to cheer.

The imaginative force of 'Strange Meeting', of course, resides in the fact that it is not a friend or an enemy that the soldier meets so much as an *alter ego*. The fascination that this idea had for the Romantic imagination is illustrated in

Rossetti's drawing 'How They Met Themselves'; it recurs in Poe's 'William Wilson' and in other tales; and it receives a particularly interesting form in Emerson's assertion 'that should he ever be bayoneted he would fall by his own hand disguised in another uniform, that because all men participate in the Over-Soul those who shoot and those who are shot prove to be identical'. The extent of Owen's familiarity with American literature is no more capable of verification than is the relationship between his pacifism and Shelley's 'Mask of Anarchy'; these parallels are cited not as authenticated sources, but as analogues indicative of a body of nineteenth-century thought to which Owen is in spirit related.

From his echoing of it in an unpublished poem, we may be certain that he knew Wilde's line 'Yet each man kills the thing he loves' and this too lies at the back of 'Strange Meeting'. The point is well made by the enemy's identification of himself with his killer in lines that are in effect Owen's own elegy, the final comment on his spiritual progress from the artificial aestheticism of the early years to the altruistic, splendid pity of these last poems:

> Whatever hope is yours
> Was my life also; I went hunting wild
> After the wildest beauty in the world,
> Which lies not calm in eyes, or braided hair,
> But mocks the steady running of the hour,
> And if it grieves, grieves richlier than here.

The enemy Owen has killed is, he suggests, his poetic self, and 'the undone years, The hopelessness' of which the enemy speaks are in one sense very personal to Owen, while in another sense they are tragically universal. Other poets had mourned the cutting-off of youth before its prime, but usually in terms of the loss to the individuals themselves or to their friends; if they envisaged the world becoming poorer they did not envisage it becoming actually worse, because tacitly or explicitly they assumed that the progress which the war had interrupted could be resumed by the survivors when it ended. Owen's vision is more penetrating and less comfortable. The war has not merely interrupted the march of mankind; it has changed its whole direction and done incalculable and irreparable damage. It is this terrible prophetic vision of a dying world embodied in this and other poems that gives Owen's work abiding relevance, but what he mourns is not merely the men themselves. Not only 'the old Happiness' but the potentialities offered by the past are unreturning, and there is truly no sadness sadder than the hope of the poet here foreseeing the disintegration of values, the retrogression of humanity, involved in this second Fall.

> Now men will go content with what we spoiled.
> Or, discontent, boil bloody, and be spilled.

.   .   .   .   .

> None will break ranks though nations trek from progress

a wise comment on history since 1918. Only the men who fought in that war had, in Owen's belief, been vouchsafed an insight into the Truth, but it was too late to put that knowledge to any constructive use. If only they could have held themselves apart from the process of disintegration, had they only had the opportunity

> To miss the march of this retreating world
> Into vain citadels that are not walled

they might, in the fullness of time, have been empowered to arrest that march and to restore the truth:

> Then, when much blood had clogged their chariot wheels,

> I would go up and wash them from sweet wells,
> Even with truths that lie too deep for taint.

Here perhaps is the last flourish of that messianic impulse which Christianity and Romanticism had combined to implant in Owen in the dedicated ideal of service to humanity that these lines express:

> I would have poured my spirit without stint
> But not through wounds; not on the cess of war.
> Foreheads of men have bled where no wounds were.

But the opportunity for such service is gone, and characteristically in one of his simplest but most effective phrases Owen indicts himself as much as anyone else for the destruction of that opportunity: 'I am the enemy you killed, my friend'.

Despite the technical maturity with which this rich complex of ideas is developed, despite the creative genius that evolved so superb a myth for its poetic purpose, it is more than the loss of a poet that one laments after reading 'Strange Meeting'. The sleep to which the dead enemy invites him is certainly

> less tremulous, less cold,
> Than we who must awake, and waking, say Alas!

for 'Strange Meeting' carries its own conviction of the irreparable loss to humanity of 'us poor lads/Lost in the ground' —irreparable not for what they were but for what they would have been, not for what they gave but for what they would have given. The epitaph that Owen chose for himself from Rabindranath Tagore is less fitting than the one which, for all its closeness to 'The Next War', he would have been too modest to borrow from a German Romantic, Heinrich Heine; 'I was a brave soldier in the war of liberation of mankind'.

CHAPTER SIX

Half-rhyme

ONE major influence that Owen exerted on the technique of English verse is, of course, his development of half-rhyme. Reviewing the 1920 edition of the poems in the *Athenæum* (10 December 1920) Edmund Blunden foresaw that 'the discovery of final assonances in place of rhyme may mark a new age in poetry', and certainly lyric poetry since then has made such extensive use of this device (known variously as half-rhyme, para-rhyme, or vowel dissonance) that it has become a characteristic of modern verse. The principle of it is familiar enough: instead of changing the initial consonant while retaining the vowel sound as rhyme does (cold/bold), the consonantal framework is retained and the vowel changed (cold/called/killed/curled). This is half-rhyme in its strictest form and as Owen regularly uses it, but it is, of course, not something that he invented. It occurs in proverbial expressions: 'Every bullet has its billet' or 'Many a mickle makes a muckle'. It is with us in the nursery in such a phrase as 'the man in the moon' or in the rhyme of the unfortunate Dr Foster who 'stepped in a puddle right up to his middle', and its frequency in such hyphenated popular formations as 'ship-shape', 'tip-top', riff-raff', 'dilly-dally', 'flip-flap', 'clip-clop', 'tittle-tattle' and so on is ample evidence of its attractiveness to the English ear. To an alert, imaginative mind interested in poetic technique any of these might be sufficient to suggest half-rhyme, and if Owen's immaturity and lack of self-confidence would have needed an impetus more positive than such casual hints there are many sources in English poetry that might have provided it.

Half-rhyme may come fortuitously into existence through a change in pronunciation of what was for the author a perfect rhyme: the eighteenth-century pairing of 'obey' and 'tea' or 'design' and 'join' are cases in point. Again, it might be suggested by what was intended merely as an eye-rhyme or as the best approximation to rhyme permitted by the sense; any collection of English hymns will provide many examples.

Deliberate use of half-rhyme, however, is to be found in three poets before Owen: Henry Vaughan, Gerard Manley Hopkins, and Emily Dickinson, but Owen's familiarity with the work of any of these three cannot be established with certainty; they are not represented in his small library which his family has preserved intact. Emily Dickinson seems the least likely influence: the two English editions of her work in 1891 and 1904 had attracted neither widespread nor very sympathetic notice and her first editors had taken such liberties in correcting and 'regularising' her prosody that the half-rhyme is much less conspicuous than in more modern—and more faithful—texts. Although the first edition of Hopkins did not appear until 1918 some of his poems were published earlier in four anthologies, but even if Owen had read these they are hardly likely to have been of direct inspiration to him, for in all the pieces so printed there are only five instances of half-rhyme and in some of those it is only internal, not end-rhyme. Nothing argues any acquaintance on Owen's part with the work of Vaughan either, but a tempting suggestion is that Owen derived half-rhyme from the same source as Vaughan and Hopkins, the Welsh. In his letters Hopkins refers to two sonnets with the explanations: 'The chiming of consonants I got in part from the Welsh which is very rich in sound and imagery', and on another occasion he mentions that 'The Wreck of the Deutschland' contains 'certain chimes suggested by the

Welsh poetry I have been reading (what they call cyn-ghanedd)'. *Cynghanedd* is an elaborate patterning of internal rhyme, alliteration and assonance which was established and classified as an essential element in Welsh versification as early as the fourteenth century but is to be found also in much earlier verse, both as internal rhyme and as end-rhyme; Hopkins tried his hand at composition of it in Welsh. He also refers, in his notebooks, to G. P. Marsh's lectures of 1860 in which Marsh drew attention to half-rhyme in early Scandinavian literature, at first internally and later as end-rhyme. It is unlikely that Owen knew either Marsh's work or Scandinavian literature, but to Marsh prob-ably belongs the credit of coining the term 'half-rhyme', a term which, incidentally, the Oxford English Dictionary does not recognise.

The possibility of a Welsh origin for Owen's half-rhyme seems further strengthened by the fact that a contemporary of his with whom he later became friendly was, just before the war, turning to Welsh poetry for metrical inspiration. In the introduction to *Collected Poems*, 1938, Robert Graves records that in about 1909 he 'adapted to English the com-plicated Welsh englyn metre, the chief feature of which is matching sequences of consonants', and he speaks of bor-rowing from the Welsh internal assonance and the rhyming of stressed with unstressed syllables. The prominence of these devices in the poetry of Vaughan was commented on by Dr. F. E. Hutchinson in his *Henry Vaughan* and in describing Owen's manuscripts I shall later indicate his conscious attention to assonance and alliteration in 'The Promisers' and 'The Kind Ghosts', although the rhyming of stressed with unstressed syllables occurs only five times in his published poems. Of half-rhyme Mr Graves wrote in a letter to me some years ago:

My first published use of it was in 1913, in my father's *Welsh Poetry Old and New*; again in the *Carthusian* 1912–14; and in my first published volume *Over the Brazier* (June 1916) which Owen had read. See 'Dying Knight and Fauns' in that book.

He did not recall Owen discussing half-rhyme with him during their acquaintance, nor did he suggest that Owen's use of it was in any way influenced by his, but what one poet has found, another may also find from the same source, especially when the other's name is Owen and his birth-place Oswestry.

More than once Owen has been hailed as a Welsh poet, especially by the Welsh, from 1928 when Ifan Kyrle Fletcher published an article on him in *Welsh Outlook* to 1944, when John Lehmann made a similar reference in a broadcast. On that occasion Owen's sister Mary at once wrote to *The Listener*:

> Both our parents were English, and though, no doubt, the name carries the implication of a distant Welsh origin, the connection is too far back to affect the fact that we are an English family. Wilfred was born at Oswestry, Salop, and would, I feel sure, have mildly resented the suggestion that he was Welsh.

Nothing on the poet's bookshelves argues a knowledge of Welsh, there is no definite suggestion of it in his published work and among the manuscripts nothing more substantial than an isolated use of the words 'plas' and 'Cymry', words familiar enough to many who make no pretensions to Welsh scholarship. It would not, then, seem likely that Owen derived half-rhyme from *cynghanedd*.

Mr Blunden's belief, hinted at in his prefatory memoir to the 1931 edition and expressed several times to me in conversation, is that Owen derived half-rhyme from the French rather than the Welsh, although he could instance no specific source. A similarly general support for such an hypothesis might be found in some remarks by Owen's friend C. K. Scott Moncrieff whose translation of the *Chanson de Roland* had been reviewed by G. K. Chesterton in *The New Witness* in December 1919. Chesterton had praised Scott Moncrieff's originality in substituting for rhyme 'a sort of rude but resonant assonance', and in a reply in the same paper the translator categorically denied any claim to originality and added:

> I should not have begun to translate Roland had not my friend Wilfred Owen, in whom I could admire and do mourn for many talents denied to myself, already made assonant verse something more than a mere joke. Nor should I have continued beyond the first dozen *laisses* had he not given an approval, based on his excellent scholarship in French and English language and on his unfaltering taste in literature generally, to the first draft of that part of my translation.

In his next paragraph Scott Moncrieff goes on to refer to Owen's 'interesting experiment in *consonance*' in his poetry and although he does not ascribe that to Owen's 'excellent scholarship in French and English' the tenor of the whole letter lends some colour to such a suggestion.

There is, however, one French poet of this century who did make deliberate use of it and in whose work Owen may have met it. Jules Romains is better known as a novelist than as a poet and even when his volumes of verse were appearing before the First World War the philosophical interest of his doctrine of Unanimism tended to eclipse his technical innovations, but his experiments with French prosody seem to me singularly close to those that Owen was to make with English. The reader especially interested in this question will find it discussed, in much fuller detail than seems desirable here, in an article which I contributed to the *Review of English Studies* in July 1950 and on which the present chapter is based.

Like Owen, Romains was not attempting iconoclasm for its own sake and sought rather to modernise than to revolutionise the traditional prosody. Both are respectful of convention when it represents a discipline, and the work of both is related to a basis of tradition: it is in matters of rhyme that both are pioneers. Romains's experimental use of *accords*, as he terms them, dates from the first decade of the century but he formulated the theory behind the practice in his *Petit Traité de Versification*, published, in collaboration with G. Chennevière, in 1923. He lists a large number of types, categories, and degrees of *accord* and he takes the principle of assonance further than Owen would have been inclined to with his *accord renversé* (*riche/chère*) and *accord renversé imparfait* (*sac/col*). While Owen's musical ear might have led him to employ such assonance incidentally he would not, I think, have systematised it as Romains does here but he would certainly have subscribed to the latter's view of the value of assonance and half-rhyme:

> Mais le propre de l'accord est de créer dans toute une suite de vers un lien harmonique à la fois plus étroit et plus continu que celui des rimes traditionelles . . . On obtient ainsi une continuité musicale à laquelle la technique classique ne pouvait pas même songer.

Such a continuity Owen achieves in the concluding stanza of 'Insensibility' (a passage to which I shall recur) by a use of half-rhyme internally as well as finally in the line, another device sanctioned by Romains.

These theories had been put into practice in two volumes of poems particularly: *La Vie Unanime* (1908) and *Odes et*

Prières (1913). In the second of these the following occur:
porte/partent/perdre, moi/mieux, murs/mort and, in one poem,
longtemps/tempes, soir/soie, tournant/maintenant and *pieds/épieu*.
Romains rarely uses half-rhyme throughout a poem as
Owen was to do, but the following are taken from *La Vie
Unanime*. The first is a particularly good example of the use
of *accords* for harmonic continuity: lines 1 and 3 are half-
rhyme, as are also 2 and 4, but there is the additional relationship between lines 1 and 2 of what Romains calls *rime
par diminution*, as there is also between lines 3 and 4:

> Les omnibus grincent et les cheminées fument;
> Les hommes sont liés par leurs rythmes confus;
> Des groupes vifs naissent, pullulent, se transforment.
> Les muscles réveillés consentent d'être forts.

('La Caserne')

Other poems show a mingling of half-rhyme with pure
rhyme such as Owen was later to use to such good effect:

> Je ne fais pas ce qu'il faudrait. J'ai peur. J'ai tort.
> Il faudrait que je bouge avant qu'il soit trop tard.
> Je suis à l'ancre; la marée emplit le port;
> Elle veut m'arracher; elle croit que je pars.

('On joue du piano, là-bas')

Such passages as these, or the conclusion to 'Le Café'
where it occurs in seven successive couplets, may well have
been responsible for suggesting to Owen's sensitive ear the
haunting cadences of half-rhyme, especially as the earliest
dated poem in which he tries out the new device is 'From
My Diary, July 1914', a poem which, if the date of its title
is the date of composition, was written in France in the year
following the publication of *Odes et Prières*.

This period at Bordeaux is the obvious opportunity for

Owen to have encountered those poems of Romains, possibly at the instigation of Tailhade who had a voracious interest in contemporary French poetry and may even have known Romains personally. This possibility is strengthened by the marked resemblance between Tailhade's views on war and those in some of these poems. Owen would not yet have attained to that intensity of feeling he was later to experience on this subject; when he did in 1917 he needed no stimulus to expression other than his own emotions and the suffering he saw around him, but the image in 'La Caserne' of the State 'feeding the barracks with fresh youth every year' and one that occurs earlier in the same poem:

> 'A l'aube, les soldats voulaient dormir encore
> Pour demeurer eux-mêmes, pour garder dans l'ombre
> Leur liberté blottie entre les draps rugueux.'

have so much in common with his conception and his method as to suggest that even in 1913 he may have been attracted to the work of Romains by a similarity of outlook as well as by an interest in technical innovation to which he could respond. If 'La Caserne' reminds the reader in many ways of 'The Send-Off' and 'Asleep', another poem from the same volume, 'Pendant une Guerre', is even more remarkable. Romains visualises a war taking place; he can read of it in the papers but can experience no feelings about it:

> La guerre me paraît aussi loin que l'histoire.
> Ce souffle d'est si caressant, je ne puis croire
> Que sa langue ait passé sur des cadavres verts.
>
> Ces hommes meurent donc dans un autre univers,
> Puisque je n'ai pas froid quand leurs veines se vident!
> Le front du firmament rêve sans une ride;

Tant pis ! Nous n'avons pas besoin de sa pitié.
Mais moi qui voudrais tant être supplicié
Lorsqu'il y a de l'âme ou de la chair qui saigne,
Faut-il que rien de toutes ces morts ne m'atteigne ?
Moi, je sais que l'on souffre, et je ne souffre pas.

In the sensuous, repulsive imagery of that third line, in the sense of the war taking place in another world (compare 'Exposure' :

> the flickering gunnery rumbles,
> Far off, like a dull rumour of some other war)

and in the whole desire to participate more actively in the universal suffering there is a very close resemblance to the later Owen.

There have been several excellent and penetrating studies of Owen published in French—indeed, he found a responsive audience across the Channel more readily than across the Atlantic—but none of these suggests the possible derivation of half-rhyme from Romains. Unless any clue exists among his unpublished papers all that can be said is that, if it has any literary antecedents and is not an original product of his inventive genius, those antecedents are more likely to have been French than Welsh or English, and that Romains is the most probable source.

II

The problem might be more easily capable of solution if one could determine with more certainty when Owen first evolved the use of half-rhyme. Mr Blunden, who has had access to more of Owen's papers than I, merely records that 'one cannot be sure when he thought out the use of assonance instead of rhymes'. The earliest use of it that can be identified is, as has been said, 'From My Diary, July 1914', where the isolating of the assonantal words suggests that the writer is experimenting deliberately with something un-familiar. There is no evidence of his using it again until February 1917 when he wrote 'Exposure'. This gap of three years seems remarkable and at first might suggest that 'From My Diary' was a later poem, the date in the title referring to the experience, not to the actual composition. The only manuscript of this poem does not settle the question; the poem itself is considerably more mature in style than any other poem of similar date that I have seen, but Mr Blunden has shown the existence of half-rhyme in at least one other non-war poem; 1915 and 1916 do not appear to have been very productive years poetically for Owen, and in any case other experiments with half-rhyme may have been des-troyed or may remain in private ownership.

One manuscript of 'The Last Word' owned by Sir Osbert Sitwell shows an unpublished use of half-rhyme and bears in one corner the date 5.3.15, but in view of the bitter note of this poem and the fact that the figures are pencilled roughly while the text is carefully written in ink I cannot accept this as the date of composition: it is a poem of which Owen would have been incapable before seeing active ser-vice. More significant is an unpublished paragraph in a letter of 6 December 1917 in which he asks Siegfried Sassoon's opinion of 'my Vowel-rime stunt' in 'Vision' and 'Wild with all Regrets', the first draft of which poem he encloses. This strengthens the conjecture that 'Vision' is an early title for 'The Show', but more interesting is the inference that the possibilities of half-rhyme had not been fully explored in discussion during their time together at Craiglockhart. It must have been in Owen's mind at that time, for Dr Frank Nicholson, then Librarian of Edinburgh University, has re-called, in the brief memoir appended to the 1931 edition,

Owen speaking of 'his idea . . . with an engaging assurance
and perhaps a touch of wilfulness'; Mr Sassoon, however,
tells me that he never saw 'Exposure' during Owen's lifetime, although he believes Owen revised the poem at Craiglockhart after reading Barbusse's '*Le Feu*' of which he finds
echoes in 'Exposure'. Presumably, then, the 'Vowel-rime
stunt' was in gestation at the end of 1917 and after Sassoon's
departure from Craiglockhart.

Of one thing there can be no doubt: the use of half-
rhyme in 'Exposure' is a great deal more subtle and more
mature than in 'From My Diary'. In spite of the freshness
and charm of the earlier poem it gives the impression that
Owen is not wholly master of his new medium. Its spas-
modic quality is consistent with a diary record, but the
regularity of its pattern—every line is end-stopped—is dic-
tated as much by an experimental, hesitant use of half-
rhyme which will not attempt run-on lines where the
assonantal word occurs elsewhere in the sentence than at the
beginning. The diction too, which in Owen's early work is
always inclined to lushness, is here largely governed by half-
rhyme; two of the words for the use of which W. B. Yeats
censured Owen, 'bards' and 'maid', owe their inclusion
rather to their assonantal than to their connotative value.
This is sometimes, though less noticeably, true of Owen's
best work in this medium; the manuscripts show that at
times his method was to jot down, marginally, lists of possible pairs of words and then build the poem round them.
In 'Exposure' there is a use of half-rhyme so much more
confident and masterly as to imply very considerable practice in the meantime. No longer does he confine himself to
monosyllabic assonance; nowhere here do we suspect a conflict between assonance and sense: 'knive us' as an echo to
'nervous' is ambitious but by no means jarring, so well does

it fit its context. Half-rhyme is even used occasionally and unobtrusively within the line (flakes/flock) or within successive lines (love/loath); the sixth stanza, by deliberately preferring the archaic 'glozed' to the more obvious 'glazed', substitutes for half-rhyme a full rhyme caught up from the 'sun-dozed' of the previous stanza and thus separates from the ugly actuality of the rest of the poem the dream of home. The artificial and rather self-conscious prominence given to the half-rhyme of 'From My Diary' is reduced in this poem by all these characteristics and also by the lengthening of the line.

This unobtrusive assimilation of half-rhyme into the structure of the poem is perfected as Owen's use of the medium develops. It is a consideration which affects his choice of metre, for only in 'Arms and the Boy', 'Wild with All Regrets', and 'Strange Meeting' does he write in half-rhymed couplets throughout. 'A Terre' begins in couplets but introduces variations in its later sections; 'Exposure' achieves its effect by an *a. b. b. a.* pattern broken by the short unrhymed fifth line, and the alternate short line of 'Miners' breaks the *a. b. a. b.* regularity. 'The Show' diverts attention still further from its half-rhyme by its presentation on the printed page which adopts the unusual course of taking the sentence as its unit and not the stanza. Its metrical basis is a half-rhymed quatrain of the *a. b. a. b.* pattern but since the sentence usually occupies two lines it gives the appearance of being divided into what might be called blank verse couplets. The monotony that too strict an adherence to this might create is avoided by occasionally lengthening the sentence to three, four, or even five lines and utilising some assonantal sounds three times instead of the usual twice. Thus the opening nine lines of the poem are really two quatrains with an additional line interpolated, not between the two, but after the first line of the second quatrain, and echoing one of the half-rhyme sounds of the first quatrain. The scheme, expressed in the conventional shorthand, is *a. b. a. b. c., b. d. c. d.* Two half-rhymed couplets are used, one of which is self-contained:

> (And smell came up from those foul openings
> As out of mouths, or deep wounds deepening.)

but the second ('straighten/flatten' at the foot of the page) by picking up the sound at the end of the preceding couplet ('eaten') in effect constitutes a triplet. The concluding lines of the poem exhibit yet another variation:

> Whereat, in terror what that sight might mean,
> I reeled and shivered earthward like a feather.
>
> And Death fell with me, like a deepening moan.
> And He, picking a manner of worm, which half had hid
> Its bruises in the earth, but crawled no further,
> Showed me its feet, the feet of many men,
> And the fresh-severed head of it, my head.

Not only in its use of the 'mean/moan/men' assonance does this passage anticipate 'Insensibility'; the telling flexibility of that poem is foreshadowed here by the change in the tempo which is effected in the last five lines by the lengthening of one line ('And He, picking a manner of worm, which half had hid') and by the separation of this from its half-rhyme by an interval of three lines instead of two, a delay which certainly heightens the impact of the dramatic identification contained in the last two words of the poem.

When in a regular metre Owen does allow half-rhyme in two successive lines those lines always contain at least eight syllables ('Futility'), generally ten ('Strange Meeting' and others), and in 'Exposure' as many as twelve. The importance of this is conveniently, if unintentionally, illustrated by two successive stanzas of an early poem.

> Has your soul sipped
>   Of the sweetness of all sweets?
> Has it well supped
>   But yet hungers and sweats?
>
> I have been witness
> Of a strange sweetness,
> All fancy surpassing,
> Past all supposing

Despite the somewhat cloying nature of its sentiment the first of these gains from its half-rhyme a dignity of movement which the second, with its almost Skeltonic jingle, lacks. This cannot be attributed merely to the feminine rhymes of the second, for in 'Exposure' feminine half-rhyme is not nearly as obtrusive nor is it in 'It is not death' where it occurs in lines equally short but with an *a. b. a. b.* pattern. In short, there is no magic in half-rhyme which makes it invariably superior to pure rhyme nor does it necessarily offer a release from the constriction of pure rhyme. Indeed, not only may half-rhyme, as in this example, produce an unpleasing jingle, but in English so few words share the requisite similarity of structure that it may become even more of a strait-jacket than rhyme. For a monosyllable such as 'war' there will be many rhymes but its half-rhymes are limited to 'were, 'wear' (or 'ware'), 'wire,' or compounds ending in those words, while there will be no half-rhyme at all for many words for which rhymes may be found in abundance. The monotony with which Swinburne re-uses such rhymes as lust/dust, rods/gods, tears/years is something which a prolonged use of half-rhyme—especially a half-rhyme as exact as Owen's—would encounter even more quickly, and the variant drafts of 'Strange Meeting' suggest, by the dogged retention of certain pairs of words, that even in that great poem the exigencies of the medium are at times near to determining the sense. Yet when all this is said, the uniqueness and the importance of Owen's peculiar use of half-rhyme remains inescapable; he gains far more than he loses by it.

It is no coincidence that of the fourteen complete poems in which he uses half-rhyme thirteen should have been written in the last twenty months of his life and of those only two ('Song of Songs' and 'The Roads Also') should be unconnected with war. These poems where he was 'not concerned with Poetry' were the ideal testing ground for this new medium which offered so happy a compromise between the ordered neatness of rhyme and the shapelessness into which unrhymed verse can so easily lapse. He would be less hesitant about experimenting in those poems because in so many of them pure rhyme would have detracted from that impression of easy, unpretentious, colloquial speech at which he aimed whereas half-rhyme, giving a less 'poetic' effect, would suit the rugged ordinariness of idiom and contribute to the naturalistic movement of the verse in such dramatic monologues as 'A Terre'. To praise the unobtrusiveness of half-rhyme may be to invite the question 'Would not blank verse have been equally effective?' One of the best answers to this—and certainly the earliest—was given by John Middleton Murry reviewing the 1920 edition in *The Athenæum* of 19 February 1921 and speaking particularly of 'Strange Meeting':

> I believe that the reader who comes fresh to this poem does not immediately observe the assonant endings. At first he feels only that the blank verse has a mournful, impressive, even

oppressive quality of its own; that the poem has a forged unity, a welded and inexorable massiveness. The emotions with which it is charged cannot be escaped; the meaning of the words and the beat of the sounds have the same indivisible message. The tone is single, low, muffled, subterranean. The reader looks again and discovers the technical secret; but if he regards it then as an amazing technical innovation, he is in danger of falsifying his own reaction to the poem. These assonant endings are indeed the discovery of a genius; but in a truer sense the poet's emotion discovered them for itself. They are a dark and natural flowering of this, and only this, emotion. You cannot imagine them used for any other purpose save Owen's, or by any other hand save his. They are the very modulation of his voice; you are in the presence of that rare achievement, a true poetic style.

III

There, of course, is the importance of Owen's half-rhyme. That Romains, Graves and Scott Moncrieff had made similar experiments suggests an awareness that this reflected better than rhyme the disintegration of values in the world around them, but for Owen it also met a more compelling, inner need. It offered a unique and perfect expression to that diffidence and lack of self-confidence that all who knew him record, and at the same time it coincided with the hesitant sense of frustration that his poetry had to communicate. It is in this way that 'the poet's emotion discovered' these assonances 'for itself' as Middleton Murry claimed, and when Murry hears in them 'the very modulation of his voice' he testifies not only to the individuality of Owen's verse but also to its dramatic quality. Half-rhyme is right for this poetry because its note of haunting uneasiness, of frustration and melancholy, accords perfectly with the theme and the mood. The pity which is in the poetry is the more emphatically brought out by it. It is not merely a matter of subconscious disappointment caused to the reader by refusing the rhyme his ear expects, while at the same time reminding him that he was expecting it; that enters into it, but the total appeal is more subtle. Michael Roberts was, I believe, the first critic to demonstrate (in the introduction to the *Faber Book of Modern Verse* 1936) how Owen deliberately chooses his vowels so that there is almost invariably a fall from a high-pitched to a low-pitched one. Thus on three occasions Owen uses 'dearth' or 'earth' as a half-rhyme for 'death', but in each case the higher-pitched 'death' comes first. In 'Arms and the Boy', however, the half-rhyme for 'death' is the still higher-pitched 'teeth' which accordingly precedes it. Again, in both 'The Show' and 'Insensibility' we have the multiple rhymes mean/moan/men and mean/immune/moans/man/mourns in that order, paralleled in 'Strange Meeting' by moan/mourn. There can be little dispute that this arrangement is deliberate, or that it does contribute to the dominant note of hopelessness that swells in these poems. Owen's ear for music is revealing itself here less obviously but to more telling effect than in his earlier poetry; so too is his capacity for taking pains with his work. The variant readings of 'Strange Meeting' are proof of that, and again illustrate the deliberateness of the falling-vowel sequence by the way in which the various versions never change the order of the rhyme-words.

Even when, as in 'Insensibility', Owen is using a rhyme scheme apparently haphazard in its irregularity, closer inspection reveals an unsuspectedly intricate pattern weaving its way through the whole; a vowel sound may be lost sight of for as many as six lines but eventually finds its echo (feet/fought and fleers/flowers in stanza I), and there is a carry-over of rhyme between stanzas which helps to knit

the whole together (march/besmirch/much in IV and V);
the varying length of the line and the much smaller proportion of end-stopped lines produce a fluidity of movement
indicative of Owen's growing mastery. The preoccupation
with form and technique which his early work reveals is
here being used to good purpose, as in the final stanza:

> But cursed are dullards whom no cannon stuns,
> That they should be as stones;
> Wretched are they, and mean
> With paucity that never was simplicity.
> By choice they made themselves immune
> To pity and whatever moans in man
> Before the last sea and the hapless stars;
> Whatever mourns when many leave these shores;
> Whatever shares
> The eternal reciprocity of tears.

The complexity of the music of this passage may be seen in
the use of 'stars' not only as a half-rhyme for 'tears' but as
a more subtle link between the two parts of the stanza by
its alliterative echo of 'stuns' and 'stones' and its role as a
loose half-rhyme for 'shores' and 'shares'. A particularly
intricate effect is also achieved by the echoing of the end-
rhyme mean/immune/man by moans/mourns/many internally; indeed, the whole phrase 'whatever moans in man'
is deliberately half-rhymed with the whole phrase 'whatever mourns when many.' In the 1920 edition the verb
'mourns' had been preferred to 'moans' in the first phrase,
and indeed Owen himself first wrote 'mourns' in both
places but his own substitution of 'moans' for the first of
these shows how carefully conceived this sound pattern is.
'Mourns' might be felt to have overtones more dignified
and tragic than 'moans' in this context, but for Owen
'moans' had its Tennysonian association with the sea and

death that he had remembered in his letter of 8 August 1917
where he uses 'the close moaning of the Bar' as a synonym
for the suffering and the

> sighs of men that have no skill
> To speak of their distress, no, nor the will!

More important than this, however, was the assonantal
gradation of 'moans' and 'mourns' which he was to use
again in 'Strange Meeting' in a similar way; in 'Insensibility' the effect that he wants at the end is not repetitive
but cumulative, the progressive deepening of tone that his
half-rhyme achieves and that develops into the evocative
sonority of the last two lines:

> Whatever shares
> The eternal reciprocity of tears.

The majestic 'reciprocity' there owes its effect partly to its
contrast with the almost monosyllabic simplicity of the
preceding lines but partly also to its echo of the internal
half-rhyme of 'paucity' and 'simplicity' six lines earlier.
The whole stanza achieves a richly contrapuntal effect in
this way.

'Insensibility' also contains an example of Owen's habit
of interspersing rhyme with half-rhyme: 'trained' in stanza
IV has a pure rhyme 'drained' as well as a half-rhyme
'trend'. The same device is used to even more subtle effect
in 'A Terre' and finds its most systematic and effective
use in 'Futility' which probably represents the fruition of
earlier experiments. If 'From My Diary' uses half-rhyme as
an added grace in a poem relying for its effect chiefly on
rhyme, we have here the logical conclusion of the movement begun there: rhyme is used in 'Futility' merely to
point a poem of which half-rhyme is the real medium.

Again the use of rhyme is to give, as in 'A Terre', a lingering effect by prolonging a note which has already been satisfied by the half-rhyme, and to give the music of the poem the 'dying fall' that accords so well with the mood. Half-rhyme is perfectly suited to the inconclusive nature of much of Owen's work, the unanswered questions, the ghosts that are so movingly raised but never laid. Of this 'Strange Meeting' is the supreme example, but the sparing and judicious combination elsewhere of rhyme with half-rhyme is unequalled for its haunting and evocative echoes.

Had Owen lived he would no doubt have explored further and in other sorts of verse the lyric potentialities of half-rhyme, of which 'The Roads Also' shows him to have been aware—more aware, indeed, than some of his early reviewers. At first the *Times Literary Supplement* (16 December 1920) seemed uncertain of Owen's intention and came very near to attributing this 'curious vagary of technique' and these 'imperfect rhymes' to bad craftsmanship. A few weeks later (6 January 1921) another notice admitted the deliberateness but questioned the success of their use: half-rhyme 'neither pleases nor is intended to please' but only reinforces the 'chastisement value' of the poems. As Middleton Murry was quick to see from the same examples, half-rhyme had a value greater than that and was certainly the product of a very real craftsmanship. Many of the poets who, in the 1930's and subsequently, have adapted half-rhyme to their own purposes have tended to blunt the edge of the instrument by using an assonantal approximation looser than Owen's. There are often very good reasons for this: I have already suggested that Owen himself could not have extended indefinitely the range of his very exact half-rhyme without either repetitiveness or distortion of the sense, and the inner logic of many of these later poems requires a half-rhyme more flexible and at times (especially for purposes of irony) even deliberately casual, as in Louis Macneice's 'Bagpipe Music'. It would be both unfortunate and unfair to allow this to obscure the aural sensitivity and poetic skill in Owen's development of half-rhyme, or to infer that his successors were lesser craftsmen than he. A close study of such a poem as C. Day Lewis's 'The Conflict' (originally published in *A Time to Dance* and included in *The Faber Book of Modern Verse*) will reveal a use of a half-rhyme as exact as Owen's, as intricate an intermixture of internal assonance and alliteration, and as skilful an integration of pure with half-rhyme; there is a structural symmetry that matches the sense in a way not immediately apparent to the reader's consciousness, and a consistent fall from high-to low-pitch vowels until in the last two stanzas the surge of a more confident tone justifies a reversal of this pattern.

To elaborate the debt of later poets to the half-rhyme Owen developed would be as tedious as to speculate on the further uses to which Owen might have put it. The 'spirit of the age' may have conditioned its evolution, but it is fortunate for the age and for English poetry that half-rhyme should have been moulded by a poet with so keen an ear for the traditional beauty of the language; fortunate, too, that circumstances otherwise hostile to him should have brought his poetic powers to such maturity of achievement at the moment when he was attaining his greatest maturity of personality and vision.

CHAPTER SEVEN

Some Problems of Text and Dating

O N 16 April 1934 *The Times* announced the acquisition
by the British Museum of an autograph collection of
Owen's poems as a gift from the Friends of the National
Libraries, 'the first manuscript of a modern author to be
bought by the Friends for presentation to a library'. In a
short notice prefacing the announcement Blunden who,
with Sassoon, had been unobtrusively instrumental in
making the bequest possible, described the collection as
'practically the whole surviving manuscript of Owen's
verse'.

Unfortunately the collection is by no means as complete
as this implies. The abundance of juvenilia does not include
eight of the poems mentioned in the memoir prefatory to
the 1931 edition, nor is there any manuscript of the following four poems or fragments printed in that text: 'It is not
death', 'Inspection', 'At a Calvary near the Ancre' and
'Le Christianisme'. A further eight poems are represented
in this collection only by texts differing from the printed
version so widely as to argue the existence elsewhere of
more fully revised manuscripts; these are 'The Unreturning', 'Shadwell Stair', 'Happiness', 'Greater Love', 'Conscious', 'The Next War', 'Sonnet: to my Friend', and 'The
End'. The collection contains only one unpublished war
poem whose completeness and intrinsic merit would justify
publication, ('The Letter, referred to at p. 69 above) whereas
two others of similar quality, 'The Soldier's Dream' and
'The Last Word', are not represented here, although Sir
Osbert Sitwell has a transcript of each. Several private

collections, varying in size, of Owen's manuscripts survive, but by no means all the titles listed in this paragraph can be thus accounted for.

This is not to minimise the undoubted value of the two volumes in the British Museum. They illustrate vividly the many difficulties that confronted the editors in their attempts to produce a definitive text from such a bewildering variety of drafts and transcripts, many never finally revised by their author; and study of these can only increase respect for the patience, the scholarly fidelity, and the intuitive poetic sympathy with which the editors approached their work. That it should now be possible for these manuscripts to be used for the infinitely easier task, which this chapter attempts, of emending some of their readings is no slight on the editors, and indeed all the corrections here proposed have been discussed with and approved by both Mr Sassoon and Mr Blunden.

A recurrent editorial problem is presented in the penultimate line of 'The Send-Off' which in the 1920 edition reads 'May creep back, silent, to still village wells' but from which Blunden omits 'still'; the fifth and latest transcribes it, strikes it out, tries two alternative epithets, and cancels both without making any final substitution. Similarly in 'The End' line 2 of the sestet contains only three feet ('My head hangs weighed with snow') although there is no other example of Owen departing from the normal length of the sonnet line. All three manuscripts of this have 'everlasting snow' but again in the latest the word is struck through but not replaced. Since in both these cases the intention seems to have been the insertion of a more acceptable adjective, not the shortening of the line, there is perhaps a case for retaining Owen's rejected word with an explanatory note. Two other small points in 'The End' are that a revision

of the latest draft makes 'sea' in the last line plural, and
that there is no manuscript authority for the capital H of
'he' (line 6) which gives a much more conventionally
Christian association than Owen intended. There may, as
already suggested, be another manuscript of 'The End'; but
this last point recalls Mrs Owen's use of an inscription from
this poem on her son's tombstone at Ors which reads 'Shall
life renew these bodies? Of a truth, All death will he annul'.
The use of capitals throughout avoids the particular crux
under discussion but the shortening of the quotation and the
change in punctuation turn the original double question into
a question with an orthodox answer diametrically opposed
to the spirit of Owen's sonnet.

The 1920 edition contained a number of printers' errors,
most of which were corrected in Blunden's edition, but
there remain one or two readings even there that are open
to question. For example, in 'Conscious' he follows Sassoon
in what appears to be a misreading in the second stanza.
'Music and roses burnt through crimson slaughter' makes
an awkward and unnecessary change of tense in the verb
from the present used throughout the poem. All three
manuscripts of this poem in the British Museum, however,
agree in reading not 'burnt' but 'burst'. Owen may have
had in mind the line of his friend Tailhade: 'L'éclat
mystérieux des roses et du sang', but in any case 'burst' is
obviously so much more satisfactory than 'burnt' that the
later manuscript which may exist elsewhere will hardly
improve upon it. Again, in 'Exposure' stanza 4, both editors
read 'deadly' where the manuscript clearly has the less
expected but perhaps more forceful 'deathly'; and in 'The
Chances' the manuscript concurs with colloquial usage in
inserting an extra negative which both editors ignore
'There ain't *no* more nor five things . . .'). The manuscript

of 'Music' has, in line 12, 'symphony' which is clearly preferable to the printed 'sympathy'; and in the 'Sonnet to a
Child' where Blunden prints 'fauns', Owen in fact wrote
'fawns' (which might suggest that the first word of the line
should be 'shy', but the collocation of 'sly' and 'fawns' in
the second stanza of 'Miners' supports the manuscript reading of 'sly').

Sometimes the problem is an awkward one of editorial
ethics. Thus the limping eighth line of 'Dulce et Decorum
Est' is obviously unpolished but the manuscripts show only
that Owen was unable to amend the line to his own satis-
faction. The only metrically sound version of it is the
original in the earlier of the two manuscripts 'Of tired, out-
stripped Five-Nines that dropped behind', and although this
was apparently cancelled at an early stage of the poem's
development perhaps the editors would have been justified
in retaining it in the text and quoting the half-revised version in a note. Again, readers may have remarked that in
anthologies the penultimate line of 'Anthem for Doomed
Youth' is sometimes printed with the phrase 'silent minds'
and sometimes 'patient minds'. The latest of the five manuscript drafts of this sonnet is a transcript in ink with some
interlinear insertions in pencil, explained by a note in
Sassoon's handwriting 'Pencilled words were written by
SS when W showed him the sonnet at Craiglockhart in
Sept. 1917'. Apparently the title was Sassoon's inspiration,
for Owen had written 'Anthem for Dead Youth', but of
all the many and fascinating changes in the successive manuscripts of this sonnet none appears to have given Owen as
much trouble as the epithet for 'minds'. With this exception
the closing two lines are in almost their final form in the
first rough draft, but more than fifteen alternatives were
considered and rejected before, in the penultimate draft and

apparently 'out of the blue', Owen produced 'silent'. Even then he was not convinced and the final transcript shown to Sassoon bracketed two alternatives: 'silent' and 'sweet white'. The second of these is scored through very decisively. (I like to think that not only were the two friends' poetic sensibilities affronted by its 'stickiness' but that their sense of humour detected the incongruous association with the 'sweet white wines' of Masefield's 'Cargoes'). 'Patient' was then pencilled in, presumably at Sassoon's instigation, but 'silent' was not deleted, either through carelessness or indecision on Owen's part. The 1920 edition, assuming carelessness, prints 'patient'; the 1931 text prefers Owen's own 'silent'. A similar problem of choice presents itself in a different aspect in connection with 'Song of Songs'. The only manuscript of this in the British Museum starts with the text as printed by Blunden but then considerably amends it in darker ink than the original. Blunden, however, has been wise in preferring to ignore these revisions in favour of the form of the poem in which Owen himself published it in *Hydra*, the Craiglockhart Military Hospital magazine, especially since the revisions do nothing to improve it. If these revisions did, in fact, take place after the publication in *The Hydra* they make an exception to one marked characteristic of Owen's emendation, the usually unerring tendency to improvement. Thus there are more than twenty recorded attempts at one line in 'Greater Love' and at least the same number of variants of the final couplet of 'The Next War' but none that one regrets his discarding. Time and again successive drafts of a poem will show a progressive movement towards the superb impersonality that characterises his best work by the gradual elimination of pronouns in the first and second person in favour of less personal constructions (this may be seen too in the draft of the Preface), or by the sort of change whereby the third line of 'Futility', 'At home, whispering of fields unsown', emerges from the original 'In Wales . . .' or the simple dignity of 'I am the enemy you killed, my friend' replaces, in 'Strange Meeting', the more limited 'I was a German conscript and your friend'.

In one other, slightly unexpected, way these manuscripts give an insight into Owen's craftsmanship. The manuscript of 'The Kind Ghosts', for example, draws attention to the careful assonantal structure of the poem by a curious system of rings, dashes, underlinings and marginal notation to bring out the sound-pattern achieved by alliteration, internal half-rhyme, and similar devices; and one draft of 'The Promisers' similarly underlines the internal rhymes.

There do not appear to be many unpublished poems that merit publication—three or four perhaps—but a definitive edition of Owen's poems which makes use of the manuscripts for textual revision, for critical comment, and even in some cases for facsimile reproduction is long overdue.

II

Owen drafted not only a Preface for his projected volume but also a Table of Contents which is reprinted in Blunden's memoir with an allusion to 'all its perplexities' but without the further commentary it merits. Not all the poems that it lists are identifiable. Some can be recognised as early variants of the published titles: 'Aliens', 'Draft', and 'Killed Asleep' are titles allotted respectively to drafts of 'Mental Cases', 'The Send-Off', and 'Asleep'. 'Nothing Happens' may with safety, though without manuscript evidence, be taken as an alternative title for 'Exposure', and 'Sonnet' (bracketed with 'Arms and the Boy' against the motive 'The unnaturalness of weapons') is unquestionably the 'Artillery' sonnet. 'Letter' and 'Heaven' are unpublished poems in the British Museum; 'The Last Word' and 'The Soldier's Dream', also unpublished, are owned by Sir Osbert Sitwell. Less easy to identify are 'Ode', 'A Ponderous Day', 'The Light', and 'The Women and the Slain'. 'Ode' may well be 'Insensibility', a poem which clearly belongs in the group where 'Ode' is entered against the motive 'Grief', and which has a formal structure unusual in Owen. 'A Ponderous Day' is perhaps a slip of the pen for 'A Ponderous Night', the opening words of one draft of the sonnet printed by Blunden as 'The Unreturning'. 'The Light' may have been an alternative to 'The Sentry'; this poem was only provisionally titled in September 1918 and 'The Light' would be applicable to the theme, especially to the final line. The omission of 'Disabled' from the list is unexpected since the three surviving drafts show it to have been a poem on which he worked with considerable care, and he sent a copy of it to Osbert Sitwell in the summer of 1918. Its affinities with 'Asleep' and 'A Terre' encourage the identification of it with 'The Women and the Slain' which Owen groups with these; the central theme of 'Disabled', which receives additional emphasis in passages cancelled in the drafts, is the callous indifference of women to the disabled soldier and since Owen frequently speaks of the disabled as similar to and in some respects worse off than the dead this title may have been intended to hint that parallel.

If these conjectures are correct only four titles that might have been expected in this list are omitted. They are 'Happiness', 'The Calls', 'Spring Offensive', and 'Smile, Smile, Smile'. The first, despite his reference to it in a letter of 8 August 1917 as including 'the *only* lines of mine that carry the stamp of maturity', may have seemed too personal for inclusion; a similar consideration may have led him to omit

'The Calls' and to list 'The Unreturning' as 'Doubtful'. The other two poems were not completed until September 1918; this need not invalidate the identification of 'The Light' with 'The Sentry' since, unlike 'Spring Offensive', that poem was at least complete on 22 September (and perhaps earlier) and Owen seems more certain of its value, though 'Spring Offensive' is the better poem. The inference, then, is that this list was drawn up before September 1918. Of the poems listed 'Miners' is known to have been written early in 1918; work was in progress on 'Mental Cases' under its earlier title of 'The Deranged' in May of that year, and 'Futility' was published in *The Nation* on 15 June.

Since the end of 1917 Owen had been stationed at Scarborough with the Reserve Battalion, and although a letter to Osbert Sitwell on 4 July states 'for fourteen hours yesterday I was at work' militarily he also suggests contributing 'some short War Poems' to the 1918 number of *Wheels*, adding that he is 'always hoping to find an hour in which to copy out and generally denebulise a few poems acceptable to' his correspondent. This obviously accounts for the number of poems of which transcripts (in many cases 'fair copies') exist in the British Museum folios written on identical paper, a fairly good quality thin quarto which he is more likely to have acquired in quantity in Scarborough than in the trenches. The Table of Contents is on this paper and so is the Preface, on the reverse of which is a draft of 'Arms and the Boy', of which poem Sir Osbert Sitwell owns another transcript on the same paper. Nowhere else does Owen use one type of paper for more than two or three poems at most, but, in all, twenty sheets of this paper can be found in the British Museum folios representing, in addition to fragments, eleven identifiable poems including a draft of 'The Sentry', 'The Calls' which I have earlier attributed on internal evidence to the Scarborough period, and 'The Kind Ghosts', of which the manuscript is dated 30 July 1918.

These conjectures imply that Owen's greatest creative phase was complete by the end of July 1918 when he was preparing to go overseas. Its beginning is marked by the composition of 'Dulce et Decorum Est' and 'The Dead Beat' at Craiglockhart in August 1917. To this period belong three-quarters of the only thirty-six of his poems that can be dated with any certainty (I tabulate these chronologically at p. 149) but in all probability many others belong to it as well. I exclude the 'Identity Disc' sonnet, dated by Blunden as 1918 (p. 104) but ascribed in his preface (p. 21) to the more likely date March 1917; but 'Strange Meeting', often thought of and referred to as one of Owen's last pieces, is included in the Table of Contents. The only important war poem that can confidently be dated earlier than August 1917 is 'Exposure' and even that poem was probably considerably re-worked at Craiglockhart. Owen's poetic achievement is remarkable enough for so young a man, but to realise from this manuscript evidence how much of it belongs to a period of about twelve months is only to wonder the more at the rapidity of his development.

CHAPTER EIGHT

The Recognition of One's Peers

OWEN was killed in action on 4 November 1918, exactly one week before the Armistice, at the age of twenty-five. A little more than two years later, at the beginning of December 1920, the volume of his poems which had been prepared from the manuscripts by Edith Sitwell and Siegfried Sassoon was published. It was reviewed by Edmund Blunden in *The Athenæum* (10 December), by Robert Nichols in *The Observer* (19 December), by J. C. (later Sir John) Squire in *The London Mercury* (January 1921) and anonymously in *The Times Literary Supplement* (16 December and 6 January) and *The New Statesman* (15 January). In addition there was a personal memoir of Owen by C. K. Scott Moncrieff in *The New Witness* (10 December 1920), an article in *The Living Age* (5 February 1921) by S. Eagle (a pseudonym of Squire's), and in the newly-amalgamated *Nation and Athenæum* (19 February 1921) the important critical essay 'The Poet of the War' (which I have quoted several times in this book) by John Middleton Murry. That Owen's poems attracted so much critical attention at a time when the posthumous publication of volumes by unknown soldier-poets was almost a daily occurrence says much not only for the quality of his poems but also for the devoted efforts of his friends on his behalf. They had, indeed, taken care that Owen was not an unknown poet when the volume appeared, for since his death they had published no less than fourteen of his poems in various periodical publications before the collected edition (see Appendix B).

That edition was reprinted in 1921 with the addition of one poem ('The End') and in the November of that year

Squire published 'Asleep' for the first time in *The London Mercury*. Meanwhile there had been some correspondence on Owen in *The Nation and Athenæum* and as literary editor of that paper Murry had followed up his article by several notes appearing sporadically in the column of miscellanea entitled 'From the Publisher's Table', of which the following is a representative example:

> We gather that the Fitzwilliam museum has denied itself the accession of Wilfred Owen's manuscripts. These were offered with the sole slight stipulation that they should be exhibited for one week of each year. The authorities at first imagined that Owen was a living poet, and we profoundly wish he was; we think that the day will come when these manuscripts will be of the first importance. Even now, are the original drafts of some of the strongest poetry produced by a mere European war not worth having at a gift?

It would be wrong, however, to suggest that the poems became at once a best-seller. Sassoon in a broadcast in 1948 gave the total number of copies printed as 2,250, of which 750 went to the United States, and there was, of course, no further printing until Edmund Blunden's revised and enlarged edition in 1931. The attitude of many readers was probably best summed up by the reviewer in the *Times Literary Supplement* in 1921 who was not only nonplussed by half-rhyme but also disturbed by such poems as 'Dulce et Decorum Est' and 'Parable':

> The suggestion is that a nation is divided into two parts, one of which talks of war and ordains it, while the other acts and suffers. We can understand how such a thought might arise, but not how it can persist and find sustenance.

If Owen had in fact written what was attributed to him, 'Yet these elegies are not to this generation', the reception of his poems would in some ways have justified the statement, for the generation to whom his work was to mean most was not his own but the younger generation growing up during the 1920's. What to the *Times* reviewer was incomprehensible to them was only too apparent. The state of European unrest that developed during the 20's and that led to the rise of Fascism in Italy and National Socialism in Germany seemed directly attributable to the Treaty of Versailles; for this and for the depression and unemployment of the 30's it was natural and not wholly unrealistic to blame the war and the older generation who seemed to have betrayed the younger out of pride, cupidity, folly, or a combination of all three. The sort of indignation underlying, for example, W. H. Auden's *Poems* of 1930 and visible especially in XXII ('Get there if you can . . .') responded readily to the more iconoclastic elements in Owen's poetry.

If, however, one of its spokesmen may be taken as typical, this generation's attitude to Owen was more complex than this. Christopher Isherwood, in his autobiographical *Lions and Shadows* (1938), attributes to them very convincingly a subconscious feeling of shame at not having been old enough to take part in the war and a consequent mental image of war as a supreme test of one's manhood; he sees himself and his contemporaries as longing to have been subjected to such a test and yet fearful that they would have been unequal to it. To such feelings, as well as to such apparently antithetical ones as those previously described, Owen provided an obvious imaginative appeal as one who, subjected to the test, had proved his manhood by the success with which he had simultaneously discharged his military duty, protested against the ubiquitous 'them' who had caused the war, and hymned the comradeship and humanity that the test had evoked in its victims. It may be in attempted emulation of this comradeship that Isherwood refers regularly to Owen in this book as 'Wilfred', often bracketing his name with that of 'Kathy' (Katherine Mansfield) in the way that Auden does in the final stanza of 'Here on the cropped grass' in *Look, Stranger!* There is something a little schoolboyish about this hero-worshipping attitude of Isherwood (though it is, after all, of his late adolescence that he is writing here), but if this seems a matter more of personality than of literature it must also be remembered how much the Auden group of poets were indebted to Owen.

II

The enlarged and textually more accurate collection of the poems published in 1931 accelerated the spread of Owen's influence, although Day Lewis's quotation of the Preface in its earlier form indicates that the 1920 edition was not completely superseded. Another important factor must have been the appearance in the influential *Criterion* of a sensitive and thoughtful essay by I. M. Parsons, the longest and fullest critical essay on Owen to have appeared up to that date (July 1931). It was in 1934 that Cecil Day Lewis in *A Hope for Poetry* took the bold step of linking Owen with T. S. Eliot and Gerard Manley Hopkins as the three poetic ancestors of the Auden group. Stephen Spender paid his tribute to Owen in *The Destructive Element* in the following year; in 1936 came Michael Roberts's important introduction to the *Faber Book of Modern Verse*; Louis Macneice acknowledged Owen's importance in his *Modern Poetry* (1938); and—not to extend the catalogue unreasonably—a very different poet of the same generation, Dylan Thomas, made his eloquent and idiosyncratic appreciation of Owen in a broadcast talk later included in the volume *Quite Early*

One Morning. 'Fame is the recognition of one's peers' Owen had told his mother in May 1918; here, it would seem, was fame in abundance.

This veneration of Owen by poets whose political pre-occupations were (except in Thomas's case) their distinguishing characteristic was no doubt what occasioned Yeats's unkind reference to Owen (in a letter to Dorothy Wellesley) as 'a revered sandwich-board Man of the revolution'. Certainly nothing in Owen's poetry or letters that I have seen identifies him with any particular shade of political opinion; the young æsthete of the pre-war years would have had little inclination to politics, nor would the author of 'Strange Meeting' have agreed entirely with Thomas Mann that 'In our time the destiny of man presents its meaning in political terms': whatever 'made fatuous sunbeams toil' was as indifferent to party politics as Hardy's Ironic Spirit. Yet when he declared 'All a poet can do today is warn' Owen linked poetry to propaganda in a way immediately attractive to the 30's.

Cecil Day Lewis was discriminating in his insistence that the only political poetry of which Owen was the real ancestor is that of the writer who 'has emotionally experienced a political situation and assimilated it through his specific function into the substance of poetry.' The political situation which Owen had 'emotionally experienced . . . and assimilated' is war, but it was not primarily as a political situation that his imagination apprehended it. Convinced only of the reality of human suffering, he came to believe passionately in two things: the iniquity of war and the potentialities of human nature if allowed untrammelled development. To the second of these beliefs the political poets of the 30's subscribed with equal fervour, though with perhaps more doctrinaire conceptions of the nature of the obstacles to that development. If they were less wholeheartedly convinced of the iniquity of war this was partly for the reasons Isherwood suggests and partly again because of their ideology: while they could in some moods see the Great War as the betrayal of the common man by capitalist economic intrigue, in other moods they could accept without misgiving the possibility of 'the next war' being for the right cause; and to many of them the Spanish Civil War in 1936 did seem so much like a war 'on Death—for Life' that their response to it, poetically and in some cases practically, was Brooke-like in its fervour and dedication: this, in Isherwood's terms, was the 'test' for which they had waited.

Certainly that war inspired some of their best poetry. Auden's 'Spain', Day Lewis's 'The Nabara' (one of the very few great modern narrative poems) and Spender's *The Still Centre* are in every way superior to their earlier political poetry which in its rhetoric had verged on the shrill and the strident. If, like Brooke, they oversimplified the issue somewhat, seeing it in straightforward terms of black and red, at least it did for a moment promise to purge them of the vestigial disillusion of the 20's. The eventual outcome of the Civil War, coupled with the casuistical attitude of the British government to it, too quickly produced a new disillusion. Each of the poets reacted differently but all of them felt an increased uncertainty and doubt of all their previously accepted standards of values. Each of them was driven back into himself, a development that Spender defined in the foreword to *The Still Centre* in terms very reminiscent of Owen's prefatory emphasis on the necessity of poetic truth to the individual experience. Gradually each of these poets felt the need to substitute an intensified belief in the individual for his earlier faith in the community, convinced by the communist defeat in Spain and the growth of Fascism in Germany and Italy that their earlier revolutionary zeal may have been too naïve. This conclusion Owen may be said to have anticipated in 'Strange Meeting', but while the poets of the 30's could accept his view of the past they were reluctant to accept his prognosis of the future until their own experience confirmed it.

Great as was their earlier enthusiasm for Owen, it is during and after the Spanish Civil War that his poetic influence on them became most important. Before that war they had been interested in what in Owen had seemed *avant-garde*: they had borrowed half-rhyme from him, they had admired his unforced colloquial idiom and the direct, anti-Romantic quality of much of his imagery. Such a simile as

> courage leaked, as sand
> From the best sand-bags after years of rain

would attract them because it was taken naturally from the immediate everyday surroundings, was forceful in the simplicity of its presentation, and yet was wholly appropriate in its context and charged with metaphorical as well as literal meaning. In the same way Auden, Spender, Macneice, and Day Lewis drew their imagery from the railways, the arterial roads, the suburbs of the civilisation around them, seeking to express a modern consciousness of good and evil in terms of the modern landscape. Yet nothing could be more foreign to Owen's method of striking at his reader's conscience than that regularly adopted by Auden in his earlier volumes. The smartness, the caustic wit, the intellectual superiority, all come from a precocity and self-confidence that Owen never had. The whole approach to the reader is different: Owen is, as he himself said, a pleader; Auden is, as he himself implied, an orator. Where one appeals to his

reader the other commands: Auden's mandatory tone is
sufficiently illustrated by the frequency of imperatives in his
poems and by the peremptory adjurations to the reader that
are not adequately excused by a desire to heighten the
urgency of communication. Too often the reader is left
with an understandable resentment at being thus brow-
beaten. Attracted by Owen's conception of the poet's service to the community, they were inclined, in their anxiety
to adapt it to their own ideology, to overlook the real significance of his words 'The Poetry is in the pity'.

With a few notable exceptions, such as Spender's 'In
Railway Halls.' 'The Prisoners', and 'An Elementary School
Classroom' or, in a rather different category, Day Lewis's
From Feathers to Iron, in their earlier poems these writers,
like Keats, seem to 'admire human nature but . . . do not
like Men'. After Spain they are more easily able to approach
the spirit of Owen's poetry, and in the third section of *The
Still Centre* Spender comes very close to Owen in such
poems as 'Port Bou' or 'Ultima Ratio Regum' where he
asks in an idiom not unlike Owen's the question that Owen
had asked:

> Consider. One bullet in ten thousand kills a man.
> Ask. Was so much expenditure justified
> On the death of one so young and so silly
> Lying under the olive trees, O world, O death?

III

Some present-day readers are inclined to be less sympathetic to Owen's pity, to see it as enervating, over-
indulged and at the core sentimental. To avoid if possible
the irrational counter-assertions of personal taste (not to say
prejudice) into which discussions of sentimentality so

rapidly degenerate, I would suggest a few relevant considerations. First, Owen's poetry is singularly free from self-pity; as Sassoon has said:

> He never wrote his poems (as so many war-poets did) to make the effect of a personal gesture. He pitied others; he did not pity himself.

Then, as I have tried to show throughout this study, pity is in his best work an active, not a passive principle. When in other war-poets pity becomes passive and sentimental it does so because they are putting forward an attitude to death rather than to life. Brooke's '1914' sonnets are not unique in seeking to arouse pity for the dead without taking realistic cognisance of why they died. If your pity is only for the dead there are no practical steps to which that pity can lead you; the temptation then is to that indulgence of sentiments for their own sake that constitutes sentimentalism. If on the other hand your pity embraces the dead, the maimed, and the living, if it is conditioned by a belief in a potentiality that they are being prevented from fulfilling, then you can try to do something about altering those conditions to prevent a recurrence of this futility and devastation. Not only does Owen's poetry say, in the words of his best friend,

> Look up, and swear by the green of the Spring that you'll never forget,

for mere recollection can become automatic and can, with the passing of time, lead to sentimentality as it did in much Armistice Day observance between the wars; at its best it communicates to his readers Owen's sense of the importance of 'the green of the Spring' as a principle of life and growth so that for them too it may become almost a moral value. Like Keats, Owen takes as his starting-point a certainty 'of nothing but of the holiness of the Heart's affections, and the truth of Imagination'; like Keats he sees these as ways to an awareness of spiritual truth which he tries faithfully to re-create in his poetry; but like Keats, also, he is at times inclined to rely too much on feelings. As his work develops this comes to be held in check by his growing mastery of language. In a phrase of Sassoon's that I have already quoted 'it was the emotional element, even more than its verbal expression which seemed to need refinement' and his increasingly confident control of verbal expression helped to refine the emotions, so that the poets of the 30's, attracted by the modernity of his idiom, came to accept his poetry as 'animated by the same *unsentimental* pity and sacred indignation' as they aimed at (the words are Cecil Day Lewis's, the italics mine). Poetry has never been divorced from feeling, but at a time when some forces at work seemed to be widening the gulf between them, it was the influence of Owen as much as anything else that brought them together. It may be that it did so with such success that we have now arrived at a critical point of balance so sensitive as to see traces of excess in what, thirty years ago, was a salutary corrective. This is, however, one of the ways in which time has validated a claim which, when Owen made it in a private letter in December 1917, may have sounded captious, even arrogant: 'I am a poet's poet'. Certainly no other war-poet has had so marked an influence on later poetry, but it is Owen's achievement also that few have retained so lasting a hold on the common reader either.

Comparisons are sometimes drawn between Owen and Isaac Rosenberg to suggest that the popular and critical assessment of their respective poetic merits have been wrong, My incidental observations will have indicated my own inclination to see them as two different kinds of poet, paralleled in the Second World War by Alun Lewis and Sidney Keyes respectively (though if value judgments are made, Lewis and Keyes both seem to me lesser poets). The distinction I am drawing can perhaps best be expressed by quotation of a passage from a letter of Rosenberg's:

> If I am lucky and come off undamaged I mean to put all my innermost experiences into the 'Unicorn'. I want it to symbolise the war and all the devastating forces let loose by an ambitious and unscrupulous will.

Rosenberg is more interested than Owen in the architechtonics of poetry, in the conscious intellectual structuring of symbols, where Owen arrives at his by a more intuitive process. To compare the confident sense of direction in Rosenberg's plans for his poetic future with Owen's wistful remark 'I am old already for a poet, and so little is yet achieved' is not to condemn Owen but to suggest that his method of approach was different. Rosenberg on another occasion remarked:

> I will not leave a corner of my consciousness covered up, but saturate myself with the strange and extraordinary new conditions of this life, and it will all refine itself into poetry later on.

If one would not expect Owen to have made that statement it is because Owen was 'not concerned with Poetry' in that sense. Both are equally dedicated, but to different things: Rosenberg, who was also a painter, to an æsthetic ideal, Owen to a social one.

It is less easy to predict what Owen's development would have been had he lived than to foresee Rosenberg's. Intellectually more mature than Owen, Rosenberg was already outgrowing the Georgians by whom Owen was so proud to be held peer: he would have been more immediately and more critically aware than Owen of the influences of Imagism, of Eliot and of the developing Yeats. The freedom of his verse-form in such poems as 'Dead Man's Dump' argues an interest in technical experiment of a nature different from anything of Owen's, and the imagery, though forceful, has the qualities desiderated in his complaint about Brooke's 'begloried sonnets' that war 'should be approached in a colder way, more abstract, with less of the million feelings everybody feels'. Owen's method is to try to work through rather than to avoid the feelings common to humanity and to aim—even if not always successfully—at control rather than coldness. The more abstract nature of Rosenberg's work may be studied in 'Daughters of War', the poem that he told Edward Marsh he believed to be his best and that supports my earlier distinction between his symbolism and Owen's: in spite of the sensuous and visual nature of its imagery, its visionary quality is clouded not so much by the obscurities in it that Rosenberg tried hard to eliminate as by the abstractness of its method. To Owen it would have seemed depersonalised, yet it has its affinities with the objectified imagism of Pound, as have such other poems as 'A Worm Fed on the Hearth of Corinth' and 'Break of Day in the Trenches'. Rosenberg's range may seem wider than Owen's—though Owen would not have wished to emulate Rosenberg's cold and abstract manner, the earthy pictorial gusto of 'Louse Hunting' would also have been out of his poetic reach—but Owen's depth of feeling and intensity of vision are, at their best, very great poetic qualities indeed. To put the whole of one's personality and energy into one's poetry, however, may be less prudent than Rosenberg's method which produces a poetry more self-contained and with a suggestion of something withheld.

The penalty of Owen's whole-hearted commitment to an immediate cause is that, had he survived the war, he would probably have needed a breathing-space in which to re-orient himself poetically, though one can be confident that he would have done it successfully. This is not saying that one is greater than the other: poetry has room for both types of poet, just as, in the 1940's, Keyes was writing with a clear consciousness of Rilke, Eliot, and Yeats, while Alun Lewis was taking a more conventional idiom and finding his own way about in it, almost as though no poetry had been written since Edward Thomas was killed.

IV

The parallel between Owen and Alun Lewis may be readily examined in terms of specific pairs of poems. 'All Day It Has Rained' is Lewis's 'Exposure', but its deliberately colloquial casualness of tone, and its preoccupation (successful on its own terms) with ephemera miss the insight of 'Exposure'. There is compassion in Lewis's poetry, there is genuine pity for suffering, but he tends too readily to identify himself with that suffering and thus misses the detachment which universalises Owen's pity. The concluding section of 'Burma Casualty' presents us with the situation of 'Conscious' and the unanswered questions of 'Spring Offensive', but then, when Owen would have broken off, Lewis goes on and the poem turns back on itself in a sentimentalisation of death that does not completely succeed.

This brief reference to Lewis is not intended as an answer to the question that one sometimes encountered between 1939 and 1945: 'Who is the Wilfred Owen of this war?' The simple answer to that is 'No one', partly for the reasons indicated in Cecil Day Lewis's tersely epigrammatic 'Where Are the War Poets?' partly because the reality of that war needed no poetic transcription by a second Owen to make it real to the civilians at home. The poet who comes closest to Owen in his fusion of pity, protest, and pleading adapted to the world of 1943 is Day Lewis in his volume *Word Over All*. The title poem itself shows something of Owen's awareness of cosmic suffering and his desire more fully to participate in it, something of Owen's diffidence at his own ability, and certainly his belief that the function of the poet is to speak for these sufferers. Unable to adopt the Christian pity that characterises Edith Sitwell's 'Still Falls the Rain', Day Lewis, like Owen, falls back on a faith in man and nature. In 'The Stand-to', as in Owen's 'Apologia' and 'The Next War' a simple faith in the quality of ordinary human beings offsets the cynicism induced by disillusion in political propaganda:

Destiny, History, Duty, Fortitude, Honour—all
The words of the politicians seem too big or too small
For the ragtag fighters of lane and shadow, the love that has
    grown
Familiar as working-clothes, faithful as bone to bone.

Blow, autumn wind, upon orchard and rose! Blow leaves
    along
Our lanes, but sing through me for the lives that are worth
    a song!
Narrowing days have darkened the vistas that hurt my eyes,
But pinned to the heart of darkness a tattered fire-flag flies.

This 'tattered fire-flag' in 'the heart of darkness' is a good symbol of the baffled idealism that is so marked in the work of both these poets. Day Lewis's 'darkened vistas' are a counterpart to the 'profound dull tunnel' of 'Strange Meeting', and there is, common to both poems, a quality of sad wisdom emotionally apprehended. Like Owen's poems,

Word Over All is the product of a particular situation (of, indeed, a particular sort of war) which it simultaneously records and transcends in its fidelity to the basic truths of human nature. These it communicates in an idiom that is direct, often colloquial, yet always imaginative and at times deeply moving in its understatement, even though at other times it may in its intensity come nearer to overstatement.

Wilfred Owen's is the poetry of a young man, instinct with the ideals, the energy, the aspirations and the disappointments of youth; for this reason, as well as for its integrity and its intrinsic qualities, it will continue to appeal to young readers and to hold its place in the tradition of English Romantic poetry. Yet more than one of these poems are anthems for doomed youth, and their mature, tragic vision of the disintegrative forces at work in the modern world guarantees their abiding interest for the older reader as well: 'Strange Meeting' is not unworthy of a place beside 'The Waste Land' and 'The Second Coming' as an imaginative diagnosis of its times. To the literary historian Owen's work may come to be of increasing value as a bridge between the poetry of the nineteenth century and that of the twentieth, but to the general reader it will commend itself for the warmth of its humanity, the spontaneous eloquence of its imagination, and the depth of its appeal to

> Whatever shares
> The eternal reciprocity of tears.

Appendices

APPENDIX A

Dates of Composition of Owen's Poems

The following table shows the month of composition of as many of Owen's published poems as can be dated with any certainty. When the month is not known the poem is given an approximate position within the year. To facilitate reference while avoiding repetition the authority for the date is given usually by quoting the page numbers in the 1931 edition (in the form e.g. 'EB 20'); where any reason for disagreeing with that date or any other evidence of date has been discussed in this book a numeral without initials refers to the appropriate page of this book; in all other cases the authority is quoted in full.

DATE		TITLE	AUTHORITY FOR DATE
July	1914	From My Diary, July 1914	EB 9 but see also 113
	1914	The Seed	EB 10 (MS dated)
	1914	The Unreturning	EB 121
Oct.	1916	Storm	EB 49
Oct.	1916–17	Music	EB 50
Jan.	1917	Happiness	EB 26
Feb.	1917	Exposure	EB 122 but see also 48 and 114
Mar.	1917	To My Friend (with an Identity Disc)	133
June	1917	The Fates	EB 79
Aug.	1917	Dulce et Decorum Est	MS dated
Aug.	1917	The Dead-Beat	51
Aug.	1917	Song of Songs	51
Aug.	1917	My Shy Hand	40

Sep.	1917	Anthem for Doomed Youth	128
		Six O'clock in Princes Street	All written on
	1917	Sonnet: to a Child	Craiglockhart
			Military Hospital
	1917	The Promisers	headed notepaper
Oct.	1917	Winter Song	EB 92
Oct.	1917	Soldier's Dream	See note below
Nov.	1917	Apologia Pro Poemate Meo	EB 86
Nov.	1917	Asleep	74
Nov.	1917	The Show	113
Dec.	1917	Wild with All Regrets	EB 91
Dec.	1917	Hospital Barge at Cérisy	EB 93
Jan.	1918	Miners	EB 125, but see also 51 which establishes January as latest date possible.
	1918	Insensibility	Patric Dickinson in a broadcast 21 Feb. 1959 (presumably in unpublished MSS)
May	1918	Mental Cases	EB 33
June	1918	Training	EB 102
	1918	Futility	52
	1918	Arms and the Boy	See note below
	1918	The Calls	56
	1918	The Roads Also	One draft written on 5 (res) Bn. Manchesters, Scarborough, headed notepaper.
July	1918	The Kind Ghosts	133
Sep.	1918	The Sentry	EB 125 but see also 74

| Sep. | 1918 | Spring Offensive | EB 125 |
| Sep. | 1918 | Smile, Smile, Smile | EB 114 |

The following tentative evidence of dating may be added:

(a) 'Greater Love'

One draft of this is written on the reverse of an unpublished poem dated 10 May 1916; though this is insufficient justification for assigning a date to 'Greater Love' its personal note and its preoccupation with death in war as a holy sacrifice might support this inference.

(b) 'Arms and the Boy', 'Disabled', 'Parable of the Old Men and the Young'.

Owen sent copies of these poems to Osbert Sitwell in July or August 1918; however, they may have been written much earlier, for the same package contained 'Mental Cases' (May 1918), 'Soldier's Dream' (October 1917), and even 'Long Ages Past' (see p. 42) which is dated 1914. That a draft of 'Arms and the Boy' is written on the reverse of the 'Preface' MS (see p. 132) strengthens the suggestion that he was working on that poem at Scarborough in July 1918, and this title is therefore included in the table above. The authority for dating 'Soldier's Dream' is an unpublished reference to it in a letter to Sassoon (27 Nov. '17) as 'The last piece from Craiglockhart'.

APPENDIX B

Dates and Places of First Publication of Owen's Poems

N.B. ★ indicates a poem not included in the 1920 edition

(a) In Owen's lifetime:

1917	In *The Hydra*	1 Sept.	p. 13	Song of Songs★
1918	In *The Nation*	16 Jan.	p. 539	Miners★
1918	In *The Nation*	15 June	p. 284	Futility
				Hospital Barge at Cérisy★

(b) Posthumously:

Containing:
    Strange Meeting
    Greater Love
    Apologia pro Poemate Meo
    The Show
    Mental Cases
    Parable of the Old Men and the Young
    Arms and the Boy
    Anthem for Doomed Youth
    The Send-Off
    Insensibility
    Dulce et Decorum Est

The Sentry
The Dead-Beat
Exposure
Spring Offensive
The Chances
S. I. W.
Futility
Smile, Smile, Smile
Conscious
A Terre
Wild with All Regrets
Disabled

Reprinted 1921 with the addition of The End.

1921   In *The London Mercury* Nov. p. 12   Asleep*

1931   *The Poems of Wilfred Owen*. Edited with a memoir and notes by Edmund Blunden. (With a portrait.) pp. vii+135 (Chatto and Windus).

Issued in the Phoenix Library with corrections but without portrait 1933.
Reprinted 1939.

Reprinted without portrait 1946.

APPENDIX C

Select Bibliography

There has been no previous monograph on Owen, but the following are the main works published in book form which contain biographical information (including extracts from letters) and significant critical comment on Owen.

No purpose would be served in listing here the uncollected articles, reviews, etc. that have appeared in periodical publications.

Edmund Blunden	Memoir and Notes in *Poems* by Wilfred Owen (London)	1931
C. Day Lewis	*A Hope for Poetry* (Oxford)	1934
David Daiches	*New Literary Values* (Edinburgh)	1936
Siegfried Sassoon	*Siegfried's Journey* (London)	1945
Osbert Sitwell	*Noble Essences* (London)	1950
V. de S. Pinto	*Crisis in English Poetry* (London)	1951

GENERAL INDEX

Persons and Periodicals mentioned in connection with
Wilfred Owen

GENERAL INDEX

INDEX

of published poems by Wilfred Owen referred to or quoted in the text

INDEX OF POEMS